T0248061

CRITICAL PRAISE FOR RON KOVIC

For *Born on the Fourth of July*

"... the most personal and honest testament published thus far by any young man who fought in the Vietnam War ... And what is so remarkable about Kovic's writing is that whereas one is perfectly prepared to forgive him occasional lapses into bitterness, self-pity, or excesses of rage, he retains the most extraordinary self-control throughout. He very patiently, meticulously, unselfconsciously defines the sort of background he came from ... [O]nly by understanding Kovic's working class credentials can one begin to comprehend the depth of betrayal he has every right to feel."   —*New York Times Book Review*

"The book details Kovic's entering of the Vietnam War as a fierce, pro-war patriot before becoming an outspoken peace activist after an injury paralyzed him and he returned home to a cold reception."
—*Rolling Stone*

"A great courageous fellow, a man of deep moral convictions and an uncompromising disposition."   —Secretary of State John Kerry

"As relevant as ever, this book is an education. Ron is a true American, and his great heart and hard-won wisdom shine through these pages."
—Oliver Stone, filmmaker

"A private and personal hell ... absolutely essential reading."
—*Minneapolis Tribune*

"Extraordinarily effective ... Kovic's unabashed expression of feelings ... becomes a form of bravery."   —*Newsweek*

"An important book ... bound to affect people ... both enthralling and dangerous."   —*Bookletter*

"This book will make you cry ..."   —*Pittsburgh Press*

"Ron Kovic has returned from the dead and given us an honest, unrefined account of his struggle."   —*Washington Post*

"Tears you to pieces ... everyone ought to read it!" —*Kansas City Star*

"A searingly realistic account written in red-hot prose . . . the most powerful book on the Vietnam War yet to be published."

—John Barkham Reviews

"*Born on the Fourth of July* tells the story of its author's transition from war hawk to protestor after being paralyzed in Vietnam, and coming home to a lukewarm reception. It's no coincidence that 'Born in the U.S.A.' tells very much the same tale."

—Billboard

"Kovic's book follows him from star high school wrestler to a patriotic American inspired by John F. Kennedy to join the marines to the traumatic 1968 wartime injury that left him paralyzed from the chest down to his emergence as an outspoken antiwar activist."

—Hollywood Reporter

"He was born in the USA—and on the Fourth of July. Bruce Springsteen narrates a foreword he wrote in the new audiobook edition of *Born on the Fourth of July*, Ron Kovic's anti–Vietnam War memoir."

—New York Daily News

"Forty years ago the Vietnam vet from Massapequa—wounded in combat and in a wheelchair ever since—published his classic war memoir, later made into a film with Tom Cruise. The anniversary edition features a foreword by Bruce Springsteen."

—Newsday

"A very moving book."

—VVA Veteran

"Rediscover: *Born on the Fourth of July*. Kovic's tale of patriotic disillusionment and poor treatment of veterans is as sadly relevant today as it was forty years ago."

—Shelf Awareness (a Great Reads selection)

"*Born on the Fourth of July* chronicles Kovic's transformation from a gung-ho soldier entering the Vietnam War to his return home as a paralyzed man. His experiences overseas, as well as the terrible way he was treated when he came back, made Kovic's book one of the antiwar movement's most celebrated works."

—Ultimate Classic Rock

"*Born on the Fourth of July* tells the story of Kovic's enlistment and how he became disillusioned with the war over time and especially after he returned home to the States. Many of the book's themes are echoed in Springsteen's hit song 'Born in the U.S.A.'"

—Asbury Park Press

"Ron Kovic's terrible tragedy is America's . . . and it has never been written 'with more force and feeling.'"   —*Los Angeles Times*

"The 1976 book, which was made into an Oscar-winning film starring Tom Cruise in 1989, details Kovic's period in the Vietnam War as a fierce pro-war patriot before he became an outspoken peace activist after an injury paralyzed him and he returned home to a cold reception."   —*NME*

For *Hurricane Street*

"Forty years after the release of *Born on the Fourth of July*, the 1976 memoir that became the 1989 Academy Award–winning film starring Tom Cruise, author Ron Kovic gives us *Hurricane Street*, a memoir about his 1974 movement to change the way Veterans Affairs hospitals cared for wounded soldiers."   —*Parade*

"*Hurricane Street* . . . [is] another raw exposé on the cost of war. The book, which [Kovic] calls a prequel, drills deep into the seventeen-day drama of a 1974 sit-in and hunger strike staged by Kovic and a band of fellow wounded veterans who took the federal building on Wilshire Boulevard by storm . . . The book is an unflinching antiwar declaration, written in blood and the sweat of too many haunted nights by a Vietnam Marine Corps sergeant who later opposed the wars in Iraq and Afghanistan."   —*Los Angeles Times*

"The author of *Born on the Fourth of July* recounts the brief 1974 movement he initiated to change how Veterans Affairs hospitals cared for wounded soldiers . . . The great strength of this book is that the author never minces words. With devastating candor, he memorializes a short-lived but important movement and the men who made it happen. Sobering reflections on past treatment of America's injured war veterans."   —*Kirkus Reviews*

"*Hurricane Street* is a powerful sequel to *Born on the Fourth of July*. It is a harrowing, poignant telling of the American Veterans Movement and its members' struggles against the government as well as themselves. The book is a must read in war and peace time. War is hell; peace can be just as brutal."   —*Manhattan Book Review*

A

DANGEROUS

COUNTRY

AN AMERICAN ELEGY

A
DANGEROUS
COUNTRY

AN AMERICAN ELEGY

RON KOVIC

BROOKLYN, NEW YORK

Published by Akashic Books
©2024 Ron Kovic

ISBN: 978-1-63614-166-4
Library of Congress Control Number: 2023933939
First printing

Some passages of the chapters "A Violent Spring," "In the Presence of My Enemy," and "Alone in Our Rooms" originally appeared in an earlier form on **truthdig**.

Akashic Books
Brooklyn, New York
Instagram, X/Twitter, Facebook: AkashicBooks
info@akashicbooks.com
www.akashicbooks.com

For TerriAnn Ferren

Table of Contents

Introduction   13

PART I: Vietnam Diary, 1967–1968   15

PART II: Breaking the Silence of the Night   111
A Violent Spring   113
The Awful Twilight   118
Breaking the Silence   120
Confessing the Sins of America   122
Kennedy   124
Expatriate   127
Return to America   136
The Sea Lodge   138
A Simple Talk in a Country Graveyard   142
Memorial Service   152
A Letter to My Mother and Father   155
Wounding   157
In the Presence of My Enemy   159
Alone in Our Rooms   163
Breaking the Crucifix   164
The Black Spot   168

PART III: The Long Journey Home   173

San Francisco: the Paris of the West   175

The Art of Healing   182

The War Is Over: a Celebration of Life   188

Tracers   193

Mona   198

A Fool for Love   212

Locked Steel Doors and Wire Windows   217

Escape from the Psychiatric Ward   222

Massapequa   225

Return to LA   237

Reckoning   240

Breakdown   245

Strange Days   248

Darkness   253

A New Dawn   256

Acknowledgments   264

INTRODUCTION

B orn on my country's birthday in 1946, I grew up in the shadow of the Cold War after the great victory of World War II. Both my mother and father had served in the navy during that war. It was where they met and were married, and we their children were to be called the baby boom. It was a beautiful time, a time of innocence, a time of patriotism, a time of loyalty, conformity, and obedience. The threat of Communism was everywhere. We did not question. We did not doubt. We believed and trusted our leaders. America was always right. How could we ever be wrong? We were the most powerful nation on earth, and we had never lost a war. But all that was to change, all that was to be shattered in Vietnam.

Deeply troubled by the growing antiwar movement and burning of an American flag in Sheep Meadow in New York City's Central Park in April 1967, I decided to set my own example of patriotism and return to Vietnam for a second tour of duty. I had arrived home that January after completing my first tour and now I was determined to go back. After submitting several request forms and three months of consistent volunteering, my orders to Vietnam finally arrived. Back then I still believed we were going to win in Vietnam, and like our fathers before us, I wanted to be a part of that victory.

Before leaving the base at Cherry Point, North Carolina, I decided to purchase a diary at the PX to record my daily thoughts and feelings during my second tour of duty. Rather than beginning each diary entry with the typical Dear Diary, I chose to begin with Dear Joe, to honor my good friend and fellow marine Joe Fucci, who I had served with at the Marine Corps barracks in Norfolk, Virginia.

Part I of *A Dangerous Country: An American Elegy* is my diary from Vietnam, beginning on July 7, 1967, and ending shortly after my wounding in January 1968; for the sake of authenticity, I have chosen to keep the diary exactly as I wrote it over half a century ago, all spelling and grammatical errors included, except for some very light editing for clarity. Parts II and III detail my long and often agonizing journey home from war as I struggled to make sense of the horrors I experienced during my second tour of duty.

PART I

VIETNAM DIARY
1967–1968

July 7, 1967
Cherry Point, North Carolina

Dear Joe,

Was promoted to sergeant today and was also told my orders for Vietnam were in. I am due in Camp Pendleton, California the 12th of August. This means I must check out and leave by next week if I want twenty days leave. The family left for Wisconsin on Friday and I might drive up and see them on my leave. Tom is home for the All-Star game. Can't believe I'm finally leaving for Vietnam after fifteen AA forms and three months of consistent volunteering. I finally made it! Jerry Malone, Ernie and myself had a "wet down" at the club last night. Jerry and I made sergeant. Have decided to begin this diary for my time in Vietnam.

July 8, 1967

Dear Joe,

Slept in today. Packed most of my gear. Saw Gunny Brown today. Called your house last night. Your dad answered.

Your pal,
Ron

July 25, 1967

Dear Joe,

Left Colden, NY today and drove 450 miles to see Karen Taylor. Got to her home only to find she and the family were up at Mountain Lake. Asked the neighbors where I might find them and they were nice enough to give me a map. Got up to Mountain Lake by 8 o'clock and met Karen. She is a beautiful girl with light reddish-brown hair and beautiful eyes. Her personality is marvelous and a remarkably wonderful sense of humor. Talked to her and found out she was engaged to Jim, says she still wants to go out. Did not tell her I was going back to Vietnam a second time. I just couldn't do it. I guess I'll have to sooner or later. She really is something. God be with you, Joe, with Saint Jude.

Ron

July 26, 1967

Dear Joe,

This morning I awoke at 0530 and Mr. Taylor and I went fishing. (No luck.) Later in the morning Karen's brother, Ray, and I caught a few perch each. Karen made breakfast for me and then we both went to the Delaware Water Gap. I took her mountain climbing and really tired her out. Something kept bothering me and I guess it was Vietnam. I finally went up to her and told her I was going to Vietnam for another year. She didn't show any emotion but I know it hit her pretty hard; from that moment on she was never the same. She just acted nice and friendly. She has much poise

and is a wonderful girl. I think if I would have met her six months ago I wouldn't be going back. But what is done is done and I shall never regret it.
Ron

July 27, 1967
Massapequa, New York

Dear Joe,

Left Karen's house today and headed back home. Karen and I went to a souvenir shop and I bought a bunch of gifts for the folks and kids, said goodbye to her, will miss her. On my way home I got lost again as usual and drove through Newark, made it back from Alpha in 4 hours to Massapequa, was wonderful to be with the family again. I love them so much. Dad bought the kids a puppy and called him Snoopy. He's really something, reminds me a lot of the Goodmans' dog Prince. It's time to say goodbye for now, Joe, will write soon. 15 days left on my leave. Saint Jude be with me.
Ron

P.S. I go to war again for one reason and one reason only: my country calls me, my country needs me, and I love my country. I will never let my country down. I leave behind much and await 13 more months of hell. Why? they ask. Why again do you go? And my retort is simply, "My country called." Oh Lord, the pain which I must suffer in these next months will make me, will mold me into a great leader in my nation's destiny. This I believe, Lord. Show me the way, the light, and the truth. I think what I do is a very small thing for the cause of freedom. No man wants to go to war, but when freedom is at stake we shall fight, we must fight!

August 11, 1967

Dear Joe,

Left New York's Kennedy Airport today at 12:30 PM, flew United nonstop to L.A. International airport. The flight was wonderful as I was able to see quite a bit of our great country. After landing in L.A. I met a few Marines heading for Oceanside. We took a cab all the way into Camp Pendleton. Cost us $5 each. (Not too bad.) Reported into staging battalion and was given a place to sleep. Word has it we should be getting processed Monday. I was talking to a LCpl (lance corporal) and he said there's 15 days training down here as it was on my last tour. Saw a movie tonight with John Wayne. I left in the middle of it. I was tired as hell from the trip. See you soon, Joe.
Take care,
Ron

August, 12, 1967
Camp Pendleton, California

Dear Joe,

Went to Oceanside today, had a Mexican dinner and saw a war movie called "The Dirty Dozen" staring Lee Marvin. It was great. Afterward went to a USO dance, about 100 Marines to every girl, got a cup of coffee and left. A lot of young kids here, most of them

out of school or boot camp. Got a lot of work to do in these next few weeks.
Ron

August 13, 1967

Went to Mass today and prayed to do outstanding in staging battalion and make it through Vietnam safe and well—received Holy Communion. Wrote a letter to Karen this afternoon; an 8 pager. Need stamps and a good close haircut. Training starts after we get processed. I should be assigned a unit tomorrow. Hope to get at least a squad or platoon of Marines. Marines run by the window chanting, "Kill, kill Viet Cong, kill!" I guess we will be doing it pretty soon. Take care, wops.
Ron

August 17, 1967

Dear Joe,

Training began yesterday. I have my own platoon now. I'm platoon sergeant. Not getting much sleep, real tired, have to keep pushing, "Junk on the Bunk" last night. Captain Kelly, our CO, inspected. Not much time for anything around here but getting ready to go into combat. Had a meeting of all my NCOs last night. My platoon guide, a Cpl Truhill, is really shaping up as a fine leader. Also second squad leader Cpl Wimbly doing fine. Cpl Wise, my third squad leader, is coming along. Told them last night we were going to have an outstanding platoon. They agreed. Take it easy, Joe.
Ron

August 18, 1967

Dear Joe,

Left for Las Pulgas and 14 days of intensive combat training to prepare for Vietnam. My platoon is really starting to come along. Most of my men are getting with the program. Wood still giving me a little trouble. He can't keep his mouth shut in ranks. Cpl Truhill and Cpl Smith and Wimbly are all doing outstanding jobs as my platoon guides and squad leaders. Gave them all a class on NCO leadership the other night and they seem to really want to go. Morale is high and most men get along with me well. I'm hard on them but it's because of where we're going.

Your pal,

Ron

August 19, 1967

Dear Joe,

Slept for more than 5 hours for the first time in 6 days—feel good. Sgt Kirby and I went into Oceanside and put some utilities in the laundry. Sgt Kirby also put in some boots. Took in two movies this afternoon, "Up the Down Staircase" and "The Sands of Iwo Jima" with John Wayne. What a movie!! Got back in at 2130 and hit the rack. Take it easy, Joe.

Your pal,

Ron

August 27, 1967

Dear Joe,

Got up at 0830 (Ah heaven!) this morning and went to 0900 Mass with my very good friend Joe Manno. His wife Cindy is doing fine and he's quite a guy. At Mass, Father Shelby presided and I've never seen a priest give such good a sermon. Slept a lot today and wrote a letter to Cpl Ryan's sister Kathy. I've only gotten one letter from home in almost three weeks and am yet to receive a letter from Karen. Also went to the club tonight and had 3 hamburgers and an egg sandwich. Talked with my third squad leader Corporal Spencer who's from Montana and another Cpl. I can't think of his name. Hit the rack.

Ron

August 28, 1967

Got up at 0400 this morning and feeling pretty good. Marched (ran) my platoon to chow then staggered back. Moved out to Papa 3 area, about a three-mile walk. The M-16 sure is quite a weapon. Most of the men enjoy it. It's lightweight and you can carry plenty of ammo. Had class today on clearing and searching a VC village, immediate action in an ambush off a truck, first aid in combat and field fortifications. The men are really hustling and doing me proud. I can truthfully say the 4th platoon is the best platoon in 3100. Wood is his same old self. Potter saw his wife and is really beginning to square away. Promising men are LCpl Tuck, Cpl Truhill, Cpl Wimbly. Cpl Smith has lost a bit of his

first-week spirit. I'm looking forward to an outstanding platoon.
Take care,
Ron

August 29, 1967

Dear Joe,

Awoke at 0500 this morning. Can't believe it. Wood wised off for the last time this morning. I wrote him up and the captain gave him 7 days restriction. Captain Kelly is an outstanding officer. He is very quiet and never says much. He backs his NCOs 100%. Congratulated me on the job I was doing for my platoon. I thanked him. Told him it was not easy getting 40 men ready for war but I'd try like hell. Tatterfield-Taylor got chewed out today. Very salty LCpl. Met Cpl Ryan, gave me his sister's address and picture, cute girl, wrote her a letter yesterday. Her name is Kathy. Haven't heard from Karen anymore. Wonder if she gave up writing? Got to keep pushing my men.
Ron

August 30, 1967

Dear Joe,

Got up at 0330 this morning. Guess what? The men have a name for me. Rock, that's Sgt Rock. I don't know if I like it or not yet. They never say it to my face, but I hear it quite frequently now. Going on "Escape and Evasion" today—will be on a 13-mile POW march and all-night escape and evasion. Breakfast this morning will

be the last time my men eat before tomorrow morning. Was very hot yesterday, 108 degrees. Never rains here in California. 10 days and we'll be leaving California for Vietnam. My men with the help of God will be ready. Take care, Joey.
Ron

August 31, 1967

Dear Joe,

POW march never came off yesterday—said it was too hot. What the hell is the Marine Corp coming to? Don't these people know it's twice as hot in Vietnam? God help us! Got up this morning at 0330. Talked to all my men last night—told them I was proud of them and we had gone a long way these past two weeks and finally we are ready as we will ever be for combat. They actually cheered me and I looked at their young faces of 18 and 19 knowing where we were headed. I told them we had a big job to do this year and to give it all for their country and the Marines. We now have an outstanding platoon and I have captured the respect and devotion of every one of my men. It is a satisfying feeling.
Take care,
Ron

September 1, 1967

Turned in our M-16s yesterday afternoon. Quite a rifle. I'd say it's the best in the world today. Would like to see a folding-stock type. Had a final "Field Day" today, then loaded aboard buses back to Camp Pendleton's 14 area. Most men feeling good about finally completing training and most really can't wait to leave for Vietnam. (If they only knew what they were in for.) Turned in all 782 gear today and got my platoon settled in our new barracks. Got a letter from Karen today. She broke her engagement with Jim and has been sick lately. Sure was great hearing from her again.

Liberty went this afternoon. Last weekend in the States for my men. Some going as far as Boston to see their folks, wives and girls for the very last time. Men all very excited and looking forward to 4-day weekend. I took Sgt Koler's duty so he could see his wife for the last weekend.
Ron

                                        September 2, 1967
Dear Joey,

Had duty all night at 3rd Rep Company office. Got relieved by Sgt Kirby and Cpl Ryan. Drank coffee all night with Cpl Bower. Talked until 1230 then slept on a table with a mattress on it. Wrote Karen a 21-page letter. (I must be destined to become a writer and not my country's leader; though I'd rather lead.) Thought quite a bit about Vietnam and living and dying. I've come to the conclusion that a man who is not afraid to die for his country and all it stands for is the most noble development of mankind. I am not afraid. I want to live for America and someday make it an even greater nation of greater people than there is today. Through God I believe this is possible. My trust is in the Lord. Went to Dis-

neyland today. It was fantastic and I had a wonderful time.
Ron

September 3, 1967
Dear Joe,

Got back from Santa Ana at 0430 this morning and took a cab from Oceanside to the base. Slept until 1130 then found out I could go to Mass this evening in Oceanside and slept until 1500. A Marine picked us up at a bus stop and drove us into Oceanside. Went to the USO. Sure is a great place. People are friendly. Truly is a home away from home. Had my laundry done and picked it up this afternoon—saw "The Magnificent Seven" with Yule Brenner. The place was packed with "Leather Necks" and we all enjoyed the rough, tough Western. Had a beer at the Playgirl Club and met two of my men . . . bought them both a Coke then headed back to Oceanside. Went to 1930 Mass in Oceanside, received Communion.
Ron

September 4, 1967
Dear Joe,

Got up this morning to set up. "Junk on the Bunk" today. Hoping for my platoon to get an "Outstanding." Met a very pretty girl at Disneyland and conversed with her for almost 45 minutes. Leaving for Vietnam in 5 more days. Sleeping on floor tonight. Most men talking about their girl or Vietnam. See you tomorrow.
Your pal,
Ron

September 5, 1967

Dear Joe,

Talley and Winter were UA off 4-day weekend. Most of my men look in good shape after the long weekend. Tatterfield came back from Boston with a bad cold. "Junk on the Bunk" inspection held this morning. Most men did ok. A few had dirty shirts on the rack. Got TB shots today. I believe they will be the last ones before we leave for Vietnam Friday. Thank God! Held 20 minutes of physical training this afternoon. My men were in very high spirits after PT. Took them for a run. We ran all over yelling and chanting, "Kill, kill, kill VC, kill—four more days—going to Vietnam . . . Kill!" People here thought we were nuts. Mail call—letter from Kathy.
Ron

September 6, 1967

Dear Joe,

Awoke at 0430. Wrote Smith up for disrespect of an NCO. For any effective unit to operate properly, discipline must be strictly enforced. Anyone can be an NCO but it takes guts and moral courage to be a good NCO. I plan to be a good one. Working party this morning. NCOs sent up in barracks. My first squad leader, Cpl Truhill, may make sergeant. He is an outstanding Marine and certainly deserves it. He would make a fine officer.
Ron

September 7, 1967

Dear Joe,

We leave for Vietnam tomorrow morning. All of 3100 were on a working party at Las Pulgas. Met Captain Clapp who was in 3/7 when I was there last year. Also met another captain who gave me an address of a major in 3rd Force Recon up in Dong Ha. Hope to get into 3rd Force and pull some patrols up in the DMZ. Told Captain Clapp I wanted to lead my own recon team on patrols. He wished me luck. Also met Donald Chichi who won the Silver Star when SSgt Kofman was ambushed last year. He looked well. Weight of all baggage made tonight. Should leave for El Toro by 0900 tomorrow morning and fly out by jet at midnight tomorrow. Should be in Vietnam next Tuesday. It's rough going up in the DMZ. Might get a Purple Heart this trip. Your pal,
Ron
P.S. Packed sea bags this evening, one for Okinawa, one for Vietnam. Told my men that we would have a "beer bust" tomorrow night—all invited. Last night in the States. Most men in high spirits. Told them I was proud of them—they were the very best. I'm being sent to the 3rd Mar Div (Third Marine Division) DMZ. Should be right in it.

September 8, 1967

Dear Joe,

Left for Vietnam this 8th day of September at 0918 in the morning. Now on a bus to El Toro. We're on our

way, finally! Arrived at El Toro at 1100, told we would
fly civilian Continental jet at midnight tonight to L.A.,
refuel, on to Wake Island Pacific (10 hr flight), eat chow,
then four hours later on to Okinawa—two days on the
"Rock," then on to Vietnam. Shook all my men's hands
today, last time together as a platoon, hell of a bunch
of fighting Marines, outstanding platoon. Read in the
news today Cong charged Marines using gas. Marines
beat them back with hand-to-hand fighting. Hell of a
war, will be there soon.
Ron

                                    September 9, 1967
Dear Joe,
    Left El Toro for aircraft, men cheering and shouting,
singing Marine Corp Hymn. I doubt in all our country's wars have men been so motivated as these men
here tonight. SSgt Andrews told me I was a "damn fine
sergeant" and said Captain Kelly had written up a letter
on my job in the staging battalion. I was very surprised
and told him it had been a pleasure working for him.
Shook many hands—said many goodbyes to my men.
They are the very best and I let them know it. In these
four weeks I have tried to instill in my men enthusiasm
for what lies ahead and this not only affected my men
but the entire unit. Left El Toro at 2100 on a Continental jet—just landed in L.A. for refuel—Wake Island 10
hours away. Went to church today and prayed for a safe
journey, now over Pacific, 2 hours to Wake.

September 10, 1967

Dear Joe,

Arrived in Okinawa at 1700 this morning—waited about 1 hour then caught a bus from the airbase to Camp Hanson—spent three hours processing and got shots. Weather here very warm—sun very hot. Were told we would be out of here and heading south to Vietnam in 24 to 48 hours. Went on liberty tonight to Fatima and BC Street. Sgt Truhill, Sgt Roy, Sgt Kirby and Cpl Wimbly went out together. Had a real great time. Sgt Truhill had a bit too much to drink and so did Sgt Roy. Got in at 3 AM—hit the rack—what a night!
Ron

September 11, 1967

Dear Joe,

Got up with a splitting headache. Lights went on at 0530 this morning and no one moved. Looked like my Leathernecks had a rough night. We make three formations a day, 0700, 1230, and 1600. Manifest for flight to Vietnam called out this morning. I was not on it. Sgt Sendry and I volunteered for the next flight out to Vietnam and got it. Would you believe I met Rodriguez and Jimmy Kelly at the snack bar today? They sure looked like they had been through hell. Rod (our M-60 machine gunner in recon during my first tour) was wounded and had quite a bit to tell me about Dunne's Raiders, also met Bill Callie and Sgt Robinson, both also going home. Said goodbye to Cpl Ryan tonight, leaving tomorrow for Vietnam.
Ron

September 12, 1967

Dear Joe,

Got up this morning at 12 midnight, left for Fatima Airbase at 0300 and boarded a C-130 (the most uncomfortable aircraft in the world) and took off at 0600 headed for Vietnam via Formosa. After 45 minutes had to turn around and come back in, radar wasn't working. Should be trying again at 1300 this afternoon. Thinking quite a bit lately, still haven't told my family I'm going to war again. Guess I'll have to sooner or later. Want to do outstanding in Vietnam and run my own patrols; can do! Landed in Danang this morning at 0819. Weather hot, was given a rack to sleep on and told to sleep wherever we could find room. Bunkers all over this place. Hit the rack.

Ron

September 13, 1967

Dear Joe,

Left Danang for Phu Bai this morning. Was told I won't be going to recon. When I got up to Phu Bai I tried to volunteer for recon, still they said no. Was told I was going to 1st Amtracs at Dong Ha. Entire airfield looked as if it had been hit by rockets and mortars.

Men up here look very tired and serious, say they get hit 5 out of 7 days with mortars and rockets. We're only 5 miles from the DMZ and there's no fooling around up here. It's a bad place. Gathered up 7 men and myself, caught a truck from the airstrip to the docks and

then the Navy took us in an LST up the Cua Viet River about a 40-minute cruise to the 1st Amtrac outpost. Looks like a tough outfit. Lost many WIA lately. Were hit by a rocket attack also lately. Volunteered for letter company. Hope and pray I get it.
Ron

September 14, 1967

Dear Joe,

Didn't get letter company. The Lord must have better plans. Was told I might go to a Letter CO in a month or so. Will be in H&S—radioman—Radio Chief is Sgt Hight, so it looks as if I won't be getting my own section for a while anyway. I don't know much about these new radios or how they work in the amtracs, nevertheless it is very interesting and I will pursue it with vigor. They talk of many wounded in this unit, mostly shrapnel wounds. A radioman got it 2 weeks ago on a sweep. He's up for the Navy Cross.

The amtracs' mission seems to be protection of the Cua Viet port and river complex which LSTs supply Dong Ha with. Sgt Hight asked if I wanted to take out an ambush patrol. I said yes but he ended up taking it. Looks like I might get in a few soon. Got mortared today, around 5 rounds. We all headed for our hole, no one hurt—too far off.
Ron

September 15, 1967

Dear Joe,

Sat radio watch all day long trying to learn what the

hell's going on here. Very confusing. This place is driving me nuts. Nothing to do. God! I wish I was in recon
or for that matter even the grunts. I figure if I'm going
to come over a second time, by God, I'd rather fight
than sit on my rear end.

So many things to learn. Radios here I've never
seen before, and of course every unit has its own way
of operating. A big operation is coming up soon.
Press people starting to come in, one is a woman,
a freelance photographer. Chow here is real good.
Showers are cold and we live in tents, some have
shrapnel holes in them from the rocket and mortar
attacks.
Ron

                              September 16, 1967
          "Ask not what your country can do for you.
              Ask what you can do for your country."
Dear Joe,

Must have asked a thousand questions today on
these new radios. I'm making some people angry but
I'm going to learn this setup if it kills me. (It might.)
Started raining today—oh Lord is it raining. Monsoon
season starting about now. Walked to chow this noon—
sunk up to my knees in slushy sand, vehicles getting
stuck. I'm all soaking wet. If you don't watch it these
monsoons can get on your mind. Rains constantly.
Stood watch most of the day. Got up this morning with
a lousy feeling. Will have to change that with a more
positive outlook. Some guy in my platoon shot his own

man on patrol the other night and the guy lost his leg.
Hell of a war!
Ron

September 17, 1967
"God give me strength."
(You wouldn't know it—
church chaplain cracked up a month ago.)
Dear Joe,
   Big operation up north of us kicked off this morning.
Lots of confusion up at the COC bunker. Top brass all
over the place. They tried to land a group from the sea
and it's so rough out there they can't get them in. Our
amtracs crossed the river and began a sweep north. B-2
patrol ran into 8-10 NVA yesterday, exchanged fire and
shot 1 NVA in the leg. A-1 came across the river to help
out B-2. They joined up and held a sweep south. Rain
coming down so hard we could not use arty. Results of
sweep unknown. I'm still learning the setup here. Re-
solved to the fact that I'm here to stay, I've decided to
get with the program and give it a hell of a try. With the
help of God I'll accomplish my mission. You wouldn't
know it but in a place like this, he knows the way.

September 18, 1967
Dear Joe,
   Today we are an island! Well almost, anyway. The
rains have completely drenched and flooded our tent
area. I looked out the tent door this morning to see 2
feet of water outside. We happen to be 2 feet 6 inches

above ground. Not much more to say about that. Rain finally stopped this morning after almost 5 straight day's rain. You have to wade up to your knees just to make a head call. Worked on radios almost all of yesterday and last night—getting better all the time. Must keep pushing and trying. May volunteer for Advisor group work to Popular Force ARVNs. Man from A Company wounded today. AP mine exploded under his amtrac. He's Alpha's radioman. I might have a new job soon. Operation still in progress. We've lost 4 amtracs to mines so far—4 wounded in action. Radios starting to come to me.
Ron

                                    September 19, 1967
Dear Joe,

    Had radio watch last night, just got off. Gunner Karbough told me I may be going to Alpha Company to replace "Stich" who was wounded yesterday. Said it would be a tough job to handle. I said I was ready. Alpha is the fighting outfit of this unit. Lots of action, many wounded, quite a challenge. This must be the Lord's plan, whatever, he knows best. Many amtracs hitting mines. You can hear it all the way back here. It shakes the whole place up. 3 or 4 more wounded yesterday. One man had 90 days left—in serious condition. A lot of time on my hands here. I ask Sgt Hight for a patrol, ambush, anything to keep me busy. B-52 strikes can be heard up north of us, they sound like a loud roar. Must really tear the hell out of Charlie.
Ron

September 20, 1967

Dear Joe,

I must learn everything I can and work my butt off. I'm going to have an outstanding section before I am through. God, this place is boring. I've been standing extra radio watch just to keep myself busy. Not much respect for military discipline around here. A lot of officers and some staff do not even refer to me as a sergeant but by my last name, Kovic. This shows very little to me. Very poor taste on their part. Gunner has said nothing about me going to Alpha Co. No one tells you anything around here, you have to find out for yourself. Rain has stopped, most area around the tent has dried up. Hope to be going to Alpha. I leave it in God's hands. Mail call! Hope I got a letter!

Your pal,

Ron

September 21, 1967

Dear Joe,

Had watch last night till 0300. Studied my political science book, also American government. Plan to go to St. John's. Will major in Political Science. Go on watch in 30 minutes. Still might be going to Alpha. Wrote a letter home and to Terry Ryan yesterday. Looking forward to an outstanding tour in Vietnam. Saint Jude is with me. Just got the word "patrol tonight," my first patrol as a sergeant. My 55th as a combat Marine. I'll be taking out 10 men. 8 semis, 2 automatics, 2 grenades

apiece. Will be setting an ambush up about 1,000 meters south of our lines. Briefing goes tonight. Lord be with me.
Ron

September 22, 1967

Dear Joe,

Got off the ambush this morning, was up all night. Saw no VC. Lost my one and only flashlight on my way to the ambush site. By the grace of God the moon was out and I could read my map by it. Called in 3 arty flares to get my position. I was about 75 meters east of where I planned. (Not bad.) Found 3 holes dug by humans, looked like mine or booby trap holes. Made no enemy contact. Actually felt good going out. Felt relieved for that matter. My navigation out and in was helped by a man who ran point for me. Damn good Marine. I took No-doze and forced myself to stay up all night. Slept in this morning—got hit by a few mortars this morning north of us. Dong Ha getting hit. B-52s raising hell up north last night. Looked like the northern lights.
Ron

September 23, 1967

Dear Joe,

Time's sure going fast around here. It will be 2 weeks here next Tuesday. I'm on edge, wish there was something to do. Told Sgt Massey I'd like a patrol any-time he gets one in. I might join a group here called the "scouts." They go out in 5-man groups, a lot like recon.

Hate sitting around! Talked to John Young last night. He has by far one of the best personalities I've seen. He's always laughing.

I sleep with my flak jacket, rifle, and cartridge close to my side in case of attack. 105 arty giving Charlie hell this morning. They're so loud they shake the whole tent up. No mail from anyone. I can truthfully say that last night before patrol I was not afraid going out. I feel a great sense of purpose and great feeling that other men as myself have defended and died for a thing called liberty. Courage surges through me when I think of our beloved President John F. Kennedy.
Ron

September 24, 1967

Dear Joe,

Feel real sick today. I've got a headache, the chills, and diarrhea. Took some aspirin, did no good. I was supposed to see the CO today about volunteering for the scouts. He didn't have time. I'll see him tomorrow. Scouts are a small 5-man group which snoops and poops around our T.A.O.R. (tactical area of responsibility) now run by the craziest sergeant I ever met. His name is Nick and he's a hard-charging Marine who doesn't give a damn. I can almost truthfully say he does not know the word fear. He's got 31 days left and I told him I sure would like to take over the scouts. He said he'd see what he could do. Scouts are sure a ragamuffin crew from Detroit to L.A., from cook to tractor rat, but with one thing in common: they want to fight! Things

are starting to look good. If I can lick this damn cold
I've got it made.
Your buddy,
Ron

September 25, 1967

Dear Joe,

Became extremely sick last night, got up, threw up
10 times, felt like I was going to die! Went to sick bay
at 0100 and had a temperature of 103.6 (burning up),
they said it was some sort of flu. Some lieutenant was
down there also, had the same thing. Slept there last
night, got up this morning and felt real weak and dizzy.
Slept most of the day, was hit by enemy artillery at 1000.
From then on we were hit around every 15-20 minutes,
5-6 rounds each. Got pretty good at grabbing my flak
gear, helmet, rifle, and running to the bunker. Takes
about 20 seconds. Last attack was at 1600. They hit real
close to us, maybe 200 feet. Most of us are more or less
angry at Charlie than scared. Enemy's arty is up near
the DMZ out of our 105's range. I'm feeling a lot better
now, will try and get some rest.
Ron

September 26, 1967

Dear Joe,

Awoke this morning and felt a lot better. Sgt Nick
informed me "scouts" may be disbanded soon. Have
decided to wait. I must learn all I can about my new
job. Now on radio watch. May still try CAC team next

month. Stood radio watch most of the day—heard we were getting a new Commo in radio with Gunner Karbough leaving in a week or two. I really can't see being stuck in a rear area outfit. I'd rather be on a one-man patrol in enemy territory than be here. But I'll have to put up with it and do the very best I can.

Your pal,

Ron

September 27, 1967

Dear Joe,

Guess what? Well I'm the new Radio Chief. Sgt Hight became platoon sergeant and I became Radio Chief. I've got some 16 men under me and quite a bit of responsibility. I talked with my section (all the others were either on guard patrol or working parties). I spent most of the day with Cpl Williams working on PM records and logs. We got a new communications officer today. I'm yet to meet him. Some men say he's awful young. I'm still hoping to be a CAP team advisor—will put in for it next month. I ask Saint Jude for the respect and devotion of all my men—volunteered for another patrol—may get it. Got a letter today from Terry Ryan's sister Kathy! Take care, Joe.

Your pal,

Ron

September 28, 1967

Dear Joe,

Awoke this morning with an outstanding outlook

. . . feel outstanding. Am looking for the impossible.
Studied last night during the movie . . . learned about
the law . . . had a really outstanding day today. My radio section has a long way to go. I never see most of
the men. They're either on guard, working parties, or
patrol. Today I began learning all the PM records with
Cpl Williams. The new captain is now in and Richie
introduced me to him. He seems very interested in his
work. Most people are saying what we need around here
is a little rank. Cpl Rod, Cpl Ford, Cpl Quelline got
their flight dates and will be leaving the battalion area
the 2nd of October—three really fine operators. CG's
(commanding general's) inspection coming up next
month.
Ron

                                    October 1, 1967
Dear Joe,

   Got a letter from Kathy today. It sure was good to
hear from someone. She sent a poem about Vietnam
her father had written and it was quite inspiring. I hav-
en't gotten any letters from Karen at all. It rained all day
yesterday and today. I spent most of the day sitting up
at the Tech shop. I asked Sgt Petty if he had any CAP
team quotas. He said no. I've started to shake things
up in the Tech section trying to square these men
away. Most of them have only two pair of utilities. I
saw Sgt Hight about it. I'm holding a rifle inspection
tomorrow at 1600. All men will have haircuts. We
cut our own hair here and wash our own cloths. The

closest civilization is 8 miles up the river at Dong Ha.
Ron

October 2, 1967

Dear Joe,

It was a beautiful morning with wind blowing cool fresh salt air. I have a great desire to get out and do something big but this outfit seems to be holding me back. I'm getting impatient. I want to go, move, do something for my country. God will lead the way.

I owe my country so much. There is so much I want to do and so little time to do it in. I am extremely proud to be fighting for freedom in Vietnam. To every generation comes its patriotic duty, and upon our willingness to sacrifice and endure rests our nation's future. I welcome the opportunity to serve my country in its hour of maximum danger, for it is the United States we fight for.
Your pal,
Ron

October 3, 1967

Dear Joe,

Sgt Petty, a friend of mine who works in the office, told me a message came in last night and the CAC team interview will go tomorrow at Dong Ha (8 miles up the river). He asked if I wanted to try for the CAC team and I said I sure would! I think my prayer is beginning to be answered. CAC stands for "combined action control" and my job would be working and living with the Vietnamese and helping them fight the Viet Cong. I'm very

enthusiastic. I think this may be the Lord's answer, I'm waiting. I picked up my SRB (service record book) from Sgt Petty and will leave on an LCU (landing craft utility) around 0600 tomorrow morning for the interview. There's a mix-up here as usual and they don't know exactly where the interview is—Dong Ha somewhere—I hope to find it by 0800. Wish me luck, Joe. I was presented the Good Conduct Medal today.
Ron

October 4, 1967
Dear Joe,
    Finally got a boat up the Cua Viet at 0900. It was an hour up the river to Dong Ha. (The most frustrating thing in Vietnam is trying to get from one place to another. It's unbelievably slow!) After much running around, finally found the place for the interview only to find out I was four hours late and had missed it. This didn't stop me. I found out where the CAC HQ was and went up to there where a GySgt gave me an interview. He told me all about CAC and their mission in Vietnam—said if I made it I'd have my own CAC company and run it pretty much by myself. I'd be in a Vietnamese village, training, sleeping and eating with Vietnamese villagers. I'd have a few Marines with me and would combine our forces to run patrols, ambushes and overall set up defenses in the village. He said he recommended me and I must wait two weeks for an answer.
Ron

October 5, 1967

Dear Joe,

Today Cpl Addington and I went to Dong Ha with one of our bad MRC-83 radio jeeps. It was an hour trip and ended up bringing the jeep into FLSG to be repaired. The jeep was in sad shape and after a few minutes driving it I became aware of the fact that we had no brakes—made it anyway. I got a letter from Mom yesterday and all is well back home. She's now a newspaper woman writing for the Massapequa Post. Cpl D. told me today the captain and gunner weren't too happy about my applying for the CAC unit. If you ever want to get anywhere in this place you're bound to get a few people angry. Anyway, my record book speaks for what I am capable of. Installed radios tonight—operation north tomorrow. I'm taking out a patrol south.

Ron

October 6, 1967

Dear Joe,

I'll be taking my patrol out at 1300 this afternoon— will be getting in around 0900 this morning. Hope for an outstanding patrol. It's quiet lately on all southern patrols—will be coming back at 0600 tomorrow morning—Saint Jude be with me. I'll have to wait on CAC 12 more days. Got 4 letters today, will have to read them when I get off patrol tomorrow.

Ron

October 7, 1967

Dear Joe,

Got off patrol this morning—most of my men very hungry and tired, walked almost 4,000 meters—made no enemy contact. We waded up to our chests in rice patties flooded by the monsoon rains. It is a great feeling of accomplishment taking out your own patrol and coming back safely. We were wet all the time. During the day we checked out sampans along the beach for VC. After taking 4 men and myself on a recon of a Vietnamese pagoda and spying on a village from a hilltop (sand dune), I set my men in an ambush off a trail near a village. Wet, cold, tired, I'd still take a patrol of 11 Marines any day—real tired, will sleep tonight.

Your pal,

Ron

October 8, 1967

Dear Joe,

Sgt Luna and I spent most of the day installing and ripping out the old amtracs. Sgt Luna is from Brentwood, L.I. and also knows George Stenson. Cpl Addington finally got a letter from his wife today after 20 days of not writing. Men in my section are Cpl Tucker, Cpl Vaughters, Cpl Demby, and LCpl Price—also Cpl Law. All on the ball but needing a little push here and there. No mail today. 9 days then possible word on CAC team programs. Hope I make it.

Take care,

Ron

P.S. Heard they're picking a new Commandant—hope it's Lew Walt.

October 9, 1967

Dear Joe,

I'm writing this by candlelight. We were hit by a storm this morning and the winds were close to 30-40 mph. Most of today was spent down at the Tech tent striping down the old ANG 7 radios and putting in the GRC 5 radios. Cpl Demby showed me how to drive an amtrac today and I drove the metal monster around a bit. CG should be coming up a few days from now. Sgt Luna sure is a nice guy. He also knows his job real well and keeps outstanding records. Captain Carlson was in the other day and said we were looking good for the CG. The rain is really pouring down my tent now. Monsoons are really with us now. Got a booster shot yesterday and felt sick all night . . . feel better. Letter from Mom.
Your pal,
Ron

October 10, 1967

Dear Joe,

We were hit by 2 or 3 artillery rounds early this morning. Raining very hard lately, tent area flooded, clear, crisp day this morning. Mom is now an editor for the Massapequa Post newspaper writing a column on school affairs. Time goes fast around here. "These are times which try men's souls. The summer solider and

sunshine patriot will in this crisis shirk from the service
of his country, but he who stands it now deserves the
love of both men and women."
Ron
P.S. I've got the feeling I'm going to do something great
over here or die trying. Just when it is going to happen
is the only question now. Courage, I have found, is a
thing which grows on you. It is a word which typifies
the American fighting man in all our wars. It is something we must all uphold over here in Vietnam regardless of all personal consequences. It's a tough order but
for our land to remain the land of the free, we must be
willing to by our actions here make it the home of the
brave.

October 11, 1967

Dear Joe,

Worked all day today down at the Tech tent moving
into the new hardback the Seabees built. You know,
a sergeant over here works just as much if not more
than the lowest-ranked private. I don't mind though.
I've learned to love good hard work. My Tech section
is beginning to shape up. Sgt Hight talked to me last
night, said many men talk about me, saying I am hard
on them, but says he does not want me to leave but
stay. He said he saw my record book and knew I had
seen my share. He asked me why I want more. He
couldn't understand. I told him it was something I
just had to do and I have a lot of faith in God as to
making it through this place. He's a damn good ser-

geant. SSgt Yates, who is Tech chief now on leave, won the Silver Star.

Your pal,

Ron

October 12, 1967

Dear Joe,

Went to Dong Ha this morning and picked up our M-83 radio jeep. On the way down by LCV I read a book called "Spearheaders," the story of Darby's Rangers during WW-2. Sure was an interesting book. Got back around 1330 to find out Cpl Bland was taking out the patrol. I was a bit disappointed but these corporals need the practice taking these patrols out. CG is coming up Saturday.

Boston tied St. Louis in the World Series, beating them 8-4. Yaz went 4-4. Final game tomorrow. Would you believe I got a letter from Karen?? She said she's been sick—sounds real good, family ok too. 2 letters from Mom. 3 new radiomen in tonight. Opening for battalion scouts. 4 days to CAC team answer.

Your pal,

Ron

October 13, 1967

Dear Joe,

Friday the 13th. Lucky day! Mom told me yesterday in her letter Tommy Law was hit in the head and sent home from Vietnam. Will need a steel plate on his skull. God be with him. Captain seems to want to find out one way or the other if I'll be leaving or not. So would I. I wish I could get back into action. I want to have my own commando outfit or just any fighting command. This place is making me soft.

Ron

P.S. St. Louis won the Series!

October 14, 1967

Dear Joe,

Awoke this morning, CG inspection of radio gear today. Rumors fly around this place (I'm used to them). Newest one is this tour is 12 months, 20 days, instead of 13 months as I spent on my last tour. Hardback tents going up all over the place. Pretty soon we will be living in them. Cpl Bland and Cpl Olsen extended an extra 6 months over here. They will go home in December for 30 days leave then back again. The fly problem around here is terrible. I heard the sprayer blew up last month—damn flies drive you nuts. I caught some kind of fungus on my back. Sgt Hight and I get along real well. He and his wife plan to move to Australia when he gets out in January. Gunner told me yesterday I had done a real fine job down at the Tech tent—said Captain thought so also. Want to do an outstanding job . . . Can do.

October 15, 1967

Dear Joe,

Cpl Kern is outside the tent heaving his guts out. He's been sick with the flu almost 6 days now. I had it when I first got here and I swear you feel like you're going to die. You get the chills, headache, then puke your guts until you spit blood. He's spitting blood right now.

This month is sure going fast, almost half over now. Results of my CAC team interview should be in the day after tomorrow. Lord, I just feel I'm going to get it. I talked to John Petty today. He wants to join the scouts, doesn't like his office job. He's got a lot of guts in my book. Tin roof tents going up all over the place. We now even have a heated shower unit. Sgt Nick caught a VC prisoner the other night (suspect). Letter from Kathy, sure is a good correspondent.

Take care,

Ron

October 16, 1967

Took out patrol last night, had a firefight with 25 VC. Wilson was killed. We took one prisoner and might have killed 4 VC. Lord, I feel so lousy about Wilson. One minute I was talking to him, the next he was shot through the neck dead. We held up in a ditch along the beach until the Reaction squad came. The major briefed me and told me my men had done a fine job out there. When Wilson got hit the doc and Huston ran out and pulled him back in under fire. I'm putting them both up for the Bronze Star. I hope they get it. I'm in sort of a daze. I couldn't sleep last night, kept seeing Wilson lying there dead. It's not hard to die over here.

Ron

October 17, 1967

God give me strength. After Wilson was killed the
other night in the firefight, we took one VC prisoner
and were bringing him back toward the beach when we
walked into 20-25 VC grouped together in a mob coming toward us. We turned around and began shooting,
bullets zinging all around us. I yelled for the men to
keep shooting as we moved back 50 feet into a long
ditch full of water. We jumped in. Wilson was last to
come in, after Doc and Huston. That's when he was
shot in the neck. Doc and Huston ran to Wilson and
dragged him in while still under fire. He died five minutes later. Fixed bayonets, then began calling in artillery.
Swift Boats came, helped out also with illumination,
Reaction platoon came up to help. Feel lousy as hell.
Ron

October 18, 1967

I'm still in somewhat of a daze, keep seeing Wilson lying
out there. I keep hearing Hill yell, "Here they come!"
and everyone shooting and running to the ditch. I'm
putting Wilson up for the Bronze Star and that will be
that. Memorial services for LCpl Wilson Friday Mass at
1500, Catholic Mass at 1400.

I am going to have to learn to live with what happened out there. It's easy to die, so easy, and just as easy
to kill, but you never forget it no matter how hard you
try. It plays over and over in my mind. I see it in my
sleep and hear it when I eat chow. Lord, help me understand why certain things must happen and why things

must be. May God have mercy on LCpl Wilson's soul.
Ron
P.S. 22 men went out tonight, machine guns—sweep
was held yesterday in the area my patrol was hit. I found
many bunkers and booby traps, one OED man blown
up by a booby trap, got it in the legs. Cpl Olsen got it in
the nose, just a scratch.

October 18, 1967

Death is common. It's hard to believe. It happens near
you and you can't believe it. All you do is realize how
easy it is to die over here. You try to forget but it plays
over and over in your mind like a broken record. You
think a lot about life and death and people and how
easy it is to die and how easy it is to kill. It happens so
quick but you remember it forever.

October 19, 1967

Dear Joe,

Sgt Luna got his flight date this morning and is now
packed and on his way. I'm now in charge of the Tech
shop and they are keeping us busy. Sgt Luna did an outstanding job and was responsible for the Tech shop getting an outstanding on the CG inspection. He said he'd
call home and tell Mom, Dad and the kids I'm ok. I
read the bible a lot lately and ask God to keep my mind
busy. Captain told me I should get the CAC team. I
hope so. I feel like a different man after the other night.
Your pal,
Ron

October 20, 1967

Dear Joe,

Memorial services for LCpl Wilson were held today in the BN—battalion area. Catholic Mass was at 1400 and Cpl Pierce and I attended. I went to Confession and received Holy Communion. Memorial services were held at 1500 for Wilson. Sgt John Petty told me his write-up on the Bronze Star was finished. I read it and it was very good. John said he should get it. I hope so. I got Wilson's wife's address and began a letter to her. I could not quite finish nor find words to express my sorrow. I'll get it out tonight.

You know, Joe, today I feel I have not only found God but have begun to find myself. I think with God and myself working together, we'll make it. I put all my trust in him. I ask for forgiveness and strength in the days ahead.

Ron

October 21, 1967

Dear Joe,

Deep patrol going south today. SSgt Winthrow taking it out—fine man. Worked today installing a new radio. We have a new gunner for our Tech section and he sure knows his job. A few of my techs said he had instructed them in San Diego. Captain asked again about my CAC unit, no word. SSgt Stafford is the new PLT sergeant and soon to be our new Comm Chief. Sgt Hight is having a little trouble getting along with him but I'm sure it will work out. I talked to Sgt Hight last night and he is quite a sergeant . . . told me he figured I had been bothered by the patrol the other night and thought I did a real fine job. I told him thanks then hit the rack. Today I ask God to show me the way and I will follow.

Your pal,

Ron

October 22, 1967

Dear Joe,

Today is Sunday morning and it is blue skies and cool in Vietnam. B-52s shook up our tent area this morning bombing up north. Just 9 days left this month. The only things you look forward to over here are chow, mail call, and sleep—to be doing nothing drives you crazy. You have to keep busy. Cpl Kern was medivaced the other day, still couldn't kick his flu. We loaded a lot of gear on trucks today, will be sending Cpl Pierce and Cpl Law down. Cpl Pierce is the sports nut in my section, Cpl Law the quiet one. I signed the final statement today on LCpl Wilson's Bronze Star. I am optimistic he will receive it posthumously. Election night in Vietnam tonight. Everyone has the ground attack jitters. Colonel expecting an attack soon. I walked into his tent tonight by mistake—felt like an idiot.

Ron

P.S. I will try and live today in Christ's name. Today God called me and I will serve him.

October 23, 1967

Dear Joe,

Cpl Demby and my good friend LCpl Young left for home this morning. They were very happy. LCpl Young, John as I called him, had one of the nicest personalities I've ever seen in a man. I won't soon forget him. CAC came in, Captain Carlson told me there was a mix-up and I'd have to wait 10 more days for an answer. I hope to get my own CAC team in a village. Will probably have to go to CAC team school in Dong Ha first.
Your pal,
Ron

October 24, 1967

Dear Joe,

Today is Tuesday, October 24, 1967 in Vietnam. I saw the major yesterday and straightened things out. I have decided that whatever happens, life must go on. I have decided to become a priest. I'm going to keep it to myself until I get home. I ask for God's help and guidance in showing me the right path. No mail today or for the past week. Sunny day today in Vietnam—not too hot. I've got a lot of things off my mind these last few days and a lot on my mind to live with. God help me in the days ahead, save me from my trouble; guide me on the right path. The Lord is my shepherd, I shall not want. Saint Jude protect me. Saint Michael be with me.
Ron

October 25, 1967

Dear Joe,

Most of today was spent working on tractors. I got a letter from Terry Ryan today and a "Sgt Rock" comic book. Terry is still in Okinawa with the 9th MEB. He is doing fine. Cpl Vaughters got very drunk tonight and pulled a .45 pistol on a man in radio relay. He cursed and swore at me, called Sgt _____ a nigger and threatened to kill him. He and Cpl Pierce got hold of some hard stuff somewhere. Captain Carlson was very angry, told me he wanted to see Vaughters in the morning. Vaughters kept on yelling and I finally took him outside and talked to him for an hour or so. He hit the rack, probably will get busted.

Ron

October 26, 1967

Dear Joe,

Cpl Vaughters got the break of his life today when the captain let him off "scot-free." Captain said he didn't want to lose a good man and didn't want to ruin it for the rest of us. Captain Carlson is very liberal with his men, he has great respect from all of us. It is a shame when a man like Vaughters ruins it for us all. Cpl Vaughters is a smart man but he has got a lot of personal problems. I'll try and work it out. It's tough being a sergeant, real tough. Captain asked me today if I wanted to go out on any more patrols. I said yes! I can't see running away from them. He said okay. Mail call in 5 more minutes, maybe a letter!

October 27, 1967

Dear Joe,

Got the word from the captain I'd be taking out a patrol south today. Muster at 0900. Mustered 11 men plus 2 scout snipers for my patrol. My assistant patrol leader is Cpl Wind Burn. Both of us went to the S-3 where Major Donovan told me where I would be going. It is a fairly deep day patrol and night ambush west of the second pagoda. I briefed my men then told everyone to be back at the guard shack at 1300. 2 grenades each and one bandolier of ammo were handed to each man. Taking out 8 semi-automatics, 2 automatics, 1 sniper rifle, 1 .45 pistol. Total of 13 men. Test fire of weapons at 1300. ETD 1330. Patrol is not far from where I got hit last week. Major said if I see them to kill them.
Ron

October 28, 1967

Dear Joe,

Got off patrol this morning. Came in at 0630. Last night was spent near the 2nd pagoda in an L-shaped ambush with Doc, Exum (the little colored radioman) and myself covering the rear. It was very quiet and as on many other patrols in this area, we saw nothing. Yesterday was spent around hill 2 (deep area) looking for Viet Cong activity on the beach and to the west of my position. Smitty checked out an old man who looked suspicious—he had his ID card. I called in a lot of artillery just to get the hang of it if we needed it. Exum got

some good practice on the radio. I kept my men in the day position until dusk then moved back to hill 3 where I got some HE and WP adjusted for our nighttime position. Came in this morning tired but feeling good.
Ron

October 29, 1967

Dear Joe,

Last night after work and chow around 1730 I just laid down for ten minutes and woke up 13 hours later feeling real good. I must have really been tired after that patrol. Have to take our M-83 jeep to FLSU at Dong Ha this morning. It's good to get out of this place for a day. I'll catch the first boat up the river then catch one back. Captain King Dixon left Vietnam last week. Read it in a newspaper. We are expected to get hit by enemy rockets next month. Went to Dong Ha today. Were hit by 2 heavy enemy artillery attacks. Bulk fuel on fire. Much destruction all around. 60 rounds landed within 100 meters of the FLSU area. Met Potter, Tackman, and Sgt Truhill, all were fine. Wood was killed last month. Hard to believe.
Ron

October 30, 1967

Dear Joe,

Talked to Sgt Hight for almost 2 hours last night. He's really a fine Marine and I enjoy talking to him. He seems to be having a problem getting used to Sgt Stafford and the captain. I hope it works out. Sgt Hight leaves on R&R for Australia next week. 7 days. Sounds real good. I feel a little bit better after taking that patrol out the other night. Did a lot of good. If it did anything, it gave me back my confidence in my ability. Waiting and praying for answer on the CAC team. Will go! Am going to wash my clothes now. Got a letter from Mom yesterday. Good to hear from them. Month is now almost over. Ron

October 31, 1967

Dear Joe,

Would you believe it, SSgt Yates walked in (winner of the Silver Star, great man). He's Tech chief and will be replacing me as chief. Feels good. Today Vice President Humphrey made a speech in Vietnam. All of us packed around the radio in our tent and we were very much moved. A tear came to my eye as I listened to the deeply moving speech supporting our role in Vietnam. He made us all proud to be Americans here in Vietnam fighting for freedom. He told us he knew it was rough but we were going to stick it out and he and our President were proud of us and had all their support. I can't express how much his speech meant to me, he is truly a great American patriot speaking the truth in a time of great crisis. I shall remember it always.
Ron

November 1, 1967

Dear Joe,

Captain went to Phu Bai for 2 days, said he would

check on the CAC team for me. I should be leaving for CAC team soon. It will be 10 days at Danang then I will be assigned my own village as a Compound Commander. I ask for the Lord's guidance in the days ahead and that I might help the Vietnamese people and bring honor upon my great country by my actions while associated with the CAC. I know God will not fail me. I am going soon and it will be a wonderful experience working hand in hand with these fine people. The Vietnamese have given many lives in this war as we have also, they have my utmost respect.

Ron

November 2, 1967

Dear Joe,

We got hit by an NVA artillery barrage early this morning. A lot of us piled into the small bunker outside our tent as the rounds screamed in. Shrapnel dropped all around, landing on top of tin roof tents with a thud. At around 0200 I awoke and didn't know what was happening until I heard a shell scream in, then another and another. I yelled, "Incoming," and my men and I ran for the bunker. I heard from the gunner, the dentist was killed; God rest his soul. Hit rack again at 3:15 AM (slept with boots on). 0700 awoke. Sandbagged Tech tent today. I've got Reaction tonight. Package from Kathy today. We eat tonight!

Ron

November 3, 1967

Dear Joe,

Most of the BN was hit pretty bad by last night's artillery attack. The dentist was killed and a few other huts really blown away. None of my men were hurt. Most of today was spent down at the Tech tent sandbagging it up. Seems everyone is building bunkers around here like crazy. (Got the Arty Party Jitters.) SSgt Yates should be picking up the Silver Star real soon. Both of us have decided to build some bunkers out on our lines. See you tomorrow.

Ron

P.S. Went to Mass today, received Holy Communion. Package from Kathy.

November 4, 1967

Dear Joe,

Talk around here is we may get hit by VC ground forces soon. SSgt Yates and I got our section out tonight and began fortifying our positions along the lines. You should see SSgt Yates, he's fantastic in his knowledge of military subjects—knows everything. He wants out of the BN battalion in the worst of ways, says he plans to ask to get out as soon as he picks up his Silver Star. Most of the men around here find ways to get chow (C-rations). Most of the time it's by "Midnight Reqs" (requisition scrounging, stealing . . . outright theft—of C-rations from the supply tent).

Ron

November 5, 1967

Dear Joe,

A lot of things happened today. Captain Carlson decided to send me to B Company after much deliberation. I'll be working under Sgt Myer who extended 6 extra months over here. B Co is known as the "Impact Area" because they get hit with so many shells during the artillery attacks. Sgt Hight, my good friend, and LCpl Hendren, who always gave me two pieces of bread on mess duty, helped load my gear in the jeep and I was off. I'll miss H&S but it's good to get out of that place for a change. Bunker down here a mess, men need supervision. We are going to have a real fine section.

Ron

P.S. Reaction tonight.

November 6, 1967

Dear Joe,

Really shaped up the bunker today, you wouldn't believe it. Got some red spray paint and went wild inside the radio bunker, sweep-down held and bunker really squaring away. Cpl Winberg is my second in command and is doing a fine job. We have 2 radio nets up, Command and BN. Plus a wire line to S-3, guard line and switchboard. It's really something when it gets busy—can really drive you crazy. I took Cpl Poole and we got a large packing crate from SSgt Yates and made a hot locker for the men. Also made a rifle rack in the bunker. Shore party took five mor-

tar rounds across the river last night—everyone hit the holes.
Ron

November 7, 1967

Dear Joe,

Sgt Hight called over the wire line last night to tell me he was leaving for Australia on R&R and asked if I wanted anything. I said no thanks and wished him well on his trip. Things around here seem to be moving so much faster than down at H&S. Even time is going by very fast. 2 more days and my 4th Marine Corp birthday will be upon us. (192 years in our proud history.) Sgt Leon is platoon sergeant. Did a lot of painting and fixing up the bunker. It's really looking outstanding. God be with me.

Sign in head, "This is a shit house, not a trash dump, please keep clean."
Ron

November 8, 1967

Dear Joe,

Put in for a transfer today to 1st or 3rd Recon BN, was turned down by First Sgt Kelly right off the bat. He asked me if I wanted to argue. "I don't argue with the Marine Corp, sir!" I said, and walked out. You should see the radio bunker, Joe, it is really squared away. All the rusty pipes are now red and it is a whole lot cleaner than when I came here. Most of my duties at B Co consist of radio and switchboard watch and general coordination of the whole section. It's a challenge and I like it. Bunker is quite small but homey. Major Burger is my CO and he is a very quiet man, very reserved, doesn't say much. Gammons is coming along well (new man). Ron

November 9, 1967

Dear Joe,

Awoke and went to chow this morning—grits and eggs as usual. On my trip to C-4 the other day, I saw 1-1 grunts moving out, and let me say they are the Marine Corp. Just finished making my own long-range antenna, and would you believe it—it works! Took 30 feet of com and ran it up one of the trees. I then hooked it to a PRC-25 radio and ran a few radio checks—works fine. First Sgt Kelly put me down in the Tech tent. (I keep telling them I'm not a Tech man, never went to Tech school!)

Today I got 4 packages from the freshmen girls at St. Agnes High School in New York. What a wonderful gift. Handed most of it out to all the men. Mom and Aunt Betts must have been behind it.

November 10, 1967

Dear Joe,

Marine Corp birthday today! Finished a book last night on Medal of Honor winner Roger Donlen—really an inspiring book about a truly great man. Today is cloudy and a bit cool in Vietnam. How-6 guns are no more than 100 meters in front of B Co and shake the whole place up when they fire. Checked guard bunker lines with Sgt Myer yesterday. He should be leaving for home on his 30-day leave (extension soon). I drink coffee very often. Matter of fact, any time I can get it. Bulldozer hit a mine up at C-4 last night. No one hurt.

I want to be a credit to my country. I want to do so much, work so hard. It's a wonderful feeling when you can dedicate every day to God and country.
Ron
P.S. Completely forgot about Mass today, will catch it next week.

                                    November 11, 1967
Dear Joe,
HOW-6s fired almost 100 rounds in about 10 minutes—what a fire mission! Although I think it was a salute to our 192nd birthday. Gammon told me this morning that he heard the top and major discussing sending me to the scouts. I couldn't believe it. Just the other day he turned my request for transfer down and now he wants to let me go to the scouts. I'm happy but found out today that "Silver Star winner" SSgt Yates also wants to lead the scouts and this might shoot down my chances. Whatever, I know God will lead me to what is good for me and my country. Had radio watch this morning. Talked with Cpl Shartel this afternoon, 2nd-tour man also. Fine NCO.
Ron

November 12, 1967

Dear Joe,

2 months here today, seems like I've been here 100 years. Felt very low today. Cpl Mangan, who won the Bronze Star, told me Major Donovan wanted me to lead the scouts. I can't believe it! Finally getting to lead my own team of scouts. Cpl Mangan said he wasn't supposed to tell me but he thought he should. I'm still being cautious of rumors so I'll just stand by and wait for God's word.

Major Donovan is as outstanding an officer as I have ever known. I have great respect for him. I owe it to him if I get my scouts. We will be the most outstanding group of Marines this battalion has ever seen. I'm going to build a team of scouts as good as any recon team there is. In God will be my trust. In him I shall not fail.
Ron

November 13, 1967

Dear Joe,

It's pouring out right now. I have never heard it rain so hard in the past 2 months—seems as if the monsoons are finally upon us. Yesterday I picked up a pair of lightweight rain trousers from Sgt Leon. They are worth a whole month's paycheck as far as I'm concerned—keep you high and somewhat dry, otherwise you'd be soaked. I checked the guard lines today during the pouring rain and everyone checked out except L.P. I feel so useless here in B Company. All I do is sit on my rear end every other day—drives me nuts. Wish I was out in the field

again—maybe soon. Greenspan made corporal. I listened to Radio Peking last night and Hanoi Hannah—a
bunch of phonies if I ever heard any. Haven't been hit
for a while.
Ron

                                    November 14, 1967
Dear Joe,
    Raining hard this morning. Wrote 2 letters last
night. One to the folks and one to Kathy. One of our
PRC-25 radios went down yesterday and I had to bring
it down to the Tech shop today. It burns me up, we're
short on radios as it is right now and antenna gear is
down to about nothing. I'll have to beg, borrow and
steal for another accessory bag just to keep us going.
Rains all the time now but really doesn't bother me. I
like to put all my problems in the Lord's hands. I know
he will come through. Sgt Stafford told me I'd be going
to the scouts. Still no real confirmation, yet things are
looking well. It's time for chow. Power has been out
here going on 3 days. Using candlelight. (Large B-52
strike up in the DMZ.)
Ron

                                    November 15, 1967
Dear Joe,
    Today my long-awaited prayer was answered and I
became NCOIC of our battalion scouts. I have 14 hard-
charging men under me now and it will be quite a job
getting this squad where I want it. Captain Hamilton,

my company commander, told me I had an outstanding reputation in this battalion and he knew I would square the scouts away. Lt Ringer is in charge of me and a fine man. Only drawback is that of these 14 men, about 10 are brand new and have never seen combat. Cpl Cozy and LCpl Farmer are my stalwarts and really with the program. I got all the men together today and told them we were going to make a name for us in the scouts, be the very best. It would be hard and whoever wanted to drop out now could, no questions asked. After that I ran them to chow and had an hour of PT. Men were very motivated and yelled freely. Will get to know every man's name by face.

Ran them through a mud puddle, told them to drop in it and they did fifty push-ups, ten sit-ups practically underwater. They loved it! (Most of them.) Saint Jude, I ask for the impossible again and that is to help build an outstanding team of scouts and do a job for my country and Corp; be recognized as an outstanding sergeant and gain the undying devotion and respect of my men. Lord answers all. Take care, Joe.
Ron

November 17, 1967

Dear Joe,

PT this morning, B team late—they will all sleep on the deck tonight. PT and ran them hard. 3 men want to quit. I work them very hard trying to make a team. Patrol tomorrow, classes today. PT'd the hell out of all my men. Drove them extremely hard today, they're really

looking sharp. I stress discipline and more discipline, speed and reflexes. Run, run, run, everyone sore all over. Cpl Cozy doing a wonderful job, right-hand man. All B team men sleep on the deck tonight—were 15 minutes late for PT. Men all trying very hard, Lord be with us, help us and protect us. 3 VC killed up north. ARVN made contact with a company of VC south of us.
Ron
P.S. Took my men out on a patrol down south near the river.

November 18, 1967
Dear Joe,

Got in this morning, saw 3 VC yesterday from a recon vantage point off a trail. Thomas was with me. I took 3 shots and the VC ran. I set my men in at hill 12 right in the middle of a large graveyard. We sat for a while, then I had Farmer and Cpl Cozy check out a trail to the east while Thomas and I checked out the one to the west. We met back at the hilltop and I called in on the radio and asked for a new night position right off the trail I checked out. We got an ok and I moved the men out at dark into the ambush position overlooking the trail. Saw nothing all night—rained and we were all very cold.
Ron

November 19, 1967
Dear Joe,

Quite a day today! Got an Australian rubber raft

from the Seabees (an old rescue type). It must be worth at least $300. Said we could have it for nothing. Scouts worked most of the day stripping her down and making her shipshape. We have six paddles and can fit all of my 10 scouts in it. I drilled and drilled my men on boat reflexes. Finally, after an hour or so, I asked Major D if we could break it in. He said yes and we made a trip across the Cua Viet River and back. We ran all the way back yelling and chanting, "Scouts, scouts, best!" Called the new raft "Raider 1."

Everyone I talk to lately asks about the scouts and if there is anything they can do to help. Captain Hamilton has helped an awful lot.

Ron

November 20, 1967

Dear Joe,

Ran the men hard this morning. My men are Cpl Cozy, LCpl Kleppen, Cpl Beeson, LCpl Farmer, PFC Molina, PFC Pons (hot head), PFC Fant, PFC Rhodes (from L.I.), LCpl Perna, PFC Thomas. That makes ten, plus PFC Sarossy, for a total of a dozen men. I'm in charge of them all and have been working their tails off trying to make a winning combat team out of them. Must have done 800 push-ups the other day. I want to make the scouts a picture of excellence. I owe it to Major Donovan who has helped us out many times and Captain Hamilton and all the others. Took a patrol south today. Men looked good. Farmer is my point and is very good. I've broken our team into 2 smaller teams. I've

got Farmer, Perna, Pons and Molina, while Cpl Cozy
has the rest—now leaving on patrol.
Ron

                                        November 21, 1967
Dear Joe,

Got off patrol this morning and it was a very good
one. Took my scouts down to the Dam Cho Chua River
about 4,000 meters south of our lines. Made no enemy
contact though we did stop 2 Vietnamese soldiers along
a trail. Most of my men want to set up an ambush along
the Dam Cho Chua River and try and get some VC. I'd
say half of my men have never been in a firefight while
Cpl Cozy, Farmer, and Kleppen are old vets. I have a
feeling inside that time is not far off. I'm surprised we
haven't been hit yet. It will give me some extra time to
drill and train my men for what is to come.

Had first aid class for all my scouts today by the
corpsmen—seems they won't be going out with us and
we will have to provide our own "buddy aid." Very tired,
up all night in ambush.
Ron

                                        November 22, 1967
Dear Joe,

Our late beloved President JFK died 4 years ago today. I read an article last night on "The Day JFK Died"
in the Catholic Digest and tears came to my eyes. I so
loved that man. Today I had Sgt Hung, the battalion interpreter, give my scouts a class on basic Vietnamese and

they did very well. This afternoon we had classes on first aid by all the corpsmen, learned how to save a man's life by cutting his throat so he can breathe, learned mouth-to-mouth and quite a bit more. The corpsmen won't be going out with us today or for that matter anymore. We're on our own now and I feel a great burden of responsibility upon my shoulders. Scouts from now on will provide their own medical attention. Major Donovan got us 2 M-79 grenade launchers and he backs me up 100%, gives me anything I need. I'm very busy lately, sweep going in 2 days. Scouts will act as recon. Patrol tomorrow.

Ron

November 23, 1967

Dear Joe,

Happy Thanksgiving. Going on patrol in about an hour. Taking out 8 men. Thomas hurt his leg on the run this morning. Pons says his back is hurting and will see the doc. Farmer is going on R&R next month to Oki and Perna will take over as point. Now have Cpl Cozy and Rhodes carrying M-79s and 30 rounds each, plus the rest of us with all automatics should put some punch into the scouts. Major D sending us on an ambush along the Dam Cho Chua River tonight. Tomorrow night we will act as a recon force and lead a company in a sweep of Vin Ha Phong just 4,000 meters south of us.

I can't help but feel great responsibility in leading these men. I know every one of them personally and will know them even better. We are starting to look like a team slowly but surely. I pray very hard to almighty God, asking him to protect every man of mine and asking him to help me make the right decisions and gain the devotion and respect of my men. I feel God's presence. I beg for his help and guidance in the weeks and months to come. Let us make our country proud of us. Lift us up, oh Lord.

Ron

P.S. I picked up a book in the supply tent. A man said don't read that, it belonged to a man killed here, (my man) LCpl Wilson. The book's title is "How to Stay Alive in Vietnam." I kept it.

P.S.S. M-16 rifles in soon, pushing and training my men very hard.

November 24, 1967

Dear Joe,

We engaged 15-20 VC in a firefight last night. It was the heaviest fire I've ever been under. I was moving the 8 of us toward the Dam Cho Chua River across a dike when a pop flare went off on our right flank. All hell broke loose and we were hit with heavy automatic weapons and machine-gun fire from our immediate right flank, bullets flying all around us, hitting very close and going overhead. A few explosions to my left front and they began to scream and laugh at us. My men were very calm, half of them this being their first time under fire. We began yelling back and cursing them out, daring them to come and get us. Cpl Cozy and Rhodes

dropped M-79s on top of them and shut them up for a while. We fired our weapons, threw out grenades, and I called in artillery. My men were very brave and I am very proud of every one of them. No one was wounded. Very high spirits. Training pays. PT today.
Ron

November 26, 1967

Dear Joe,

Took out a patrol today south of hill 2 near Vin Ha Phong (VC area). No enemy contact. Found a large bloodstain in the sand with a man's bloody garments all around hill 3 area. Evidence shows he was dragged away. Naval gun shell must have got him. LCpl Farmer is my point man and he is outstanding, very smart and quick. Perna is his backup. Pons giving me trouble. 19-year-old green kid thinks he knows it all. He's been here one month. I can't believe some of these new kids we're getting. Next month will be my 16th month of combat in Vietnam. Average age of my team is about 19 years old. (Would you believe it?) I'm the 21-year-"old man." Set in around hill 3, cool and windy.
Ron

November 27, 1967

Dear Joe,

Came in this morn from patrol, felt real good. I've picked up smoking a cigarette every time we come in from patrol. (Bad habit.) God, how getting shot at can change a man's outlook on life. Lt Hectus and MSgt

Creeden's Reaction platoon gave us a hand the other night. They ended up leaving us out there through the cold and rain for the rest of the night. I went to my knees in a hole on top of hill 3 in a pouring rain and thanked God from the bottom of my heart for helping us and giving me courage when I needed it most. Major D shook my hand when I came in and said we had done a fine job. He was proud of us all. Told me PFs (Popular Forces) were part of the element which hit us. Possible VC PFs. Hell of a war.
Ron

November 28, 1967

Dear Joey,
This morning most of my men were busy taking C.E.D. tests while the others were in working parties. Major Burger from B Company has a tractor recon of Vin Ha Phong this afternoon. Artillery procedure class. Major Donovan told me I did an outstanding job calling in the arty the other night. All my scouts now wearing our black berets and they certainly look sharp. They worked hard for them and will have to work even harder to keep them. We got down to BCO at 1500 and jumped on the amtracs where we reconned out Vin Ha Phong. It was the same area I got hit at back in October. Came in from recon at 1600. My men are moving out at 2000 tonight for our first leg of the recon mission. It's now 2015. Painted-black faces and berets, now moving out.
Ron

November 29, 1967

Dear Joe,

Stayed on hill 3 area until 0200 hrs when we met Major B and his tractor-blocking force. Moved my men out down the tree line to the stream in back of Vin Ha Phong. Crossed many flooded open areas. 9 of us finally made it to the stream and moved to the beach where we set up a 360 and I signaled to Major B's force which was moving down the beach (about 40 men). We linked up around 0530 and we (scouts) guided them down the path north of the stream and set in waiting for light and the sweep on Vin Ha Phong. Sweep held, approx. 15 booby traps found, a few punji stakes also. Came in dead tired. Up all night. Flopped on my rack tired. Woke up 8 hours later.

Ron

November 30, 1967

Dear Joe,

Lord, I am so busy I can't believe it. If we're not training we're in the field on patrol. Time going very fast now. Word today is "patrol south," most of the men complaining that it's not our turn to go out again. Boy, wherever they want us to go, we go! As far as I'm concerned, I can see their point though. They're all pretty bent from the other night. Major D wants me to check out the northern edge of Vin Ha Phong. Moving out at 1500—8 automatics, 2 M-78 grenade launchers, black berets. Picked up 2 suspects at the vill and sent them back to the BN area. Went back out and set in at hill 3 area for the night.

December 1, 1967

Dear Joe,

Came in this morning. It was a very cold, wet, totally miserable night. All the men drenched to the skin. Laid in the sand all night with the rains driving on us and cold winds whipping up—I felt like cursing the weather but knew it would do no good. And anyway, I asked to come here a second time. Came in and cleaned my weapon most of the morning, then got a debriefing. Just when I was getting ready to sack out, Lt Ringer asked me to assist him as pay clerk. Lord!

Went to Mass today and received Holy Communion. Major D said my scouts would be moving north for a few patrols soon. 5 men from A Co wounded up north today. It's hot up there. Sent check home.
Ron

December 2, 1967

Dear Joe,

No PT this morning. Got everyone in the B tent to move all their gear to the A tent. Very crowded—10 men in my tent. Should help to build more teamwork and esprit d'corps. 4 men on wire detail this afternoon. 1 man killed, 5 others wounded from A Co. God rest his soul.

A letter from Audrey Ryan (no relation to Kathy) today. She is a good friend of the family. Letter from Mom

today and pictures of our family, the Khares family, and Goodman's. All looking well. Wrote a few letters last night to the folks ($300 check). Kathy Ryan, Terry Ryan (brother), Karen T, and Tom. Got a letter from Tom yesterday also. He did a pirouette on the P-bars and is going out for wrestling. Lights just went out.
Ron

December 3, 1967

Dear Joe,

Patrol tonight—will be a short one down near hill 3. I now have a total of 12 men under my command (the dirty dozen). They all wear their black berets now and are really impressive. Major D wants to patrol us up north for the next few days. Package from the VFW. God bless them.
Ron

December 4, 1967

Dear Joe,

Got off patrol this morning, wet all night, saw nothing. Our lines were quite active as they spotted 10-15 VC trying to infiltrate our lines. We just sat out on patrol waiting for them to come toward us. Letter from Lou Ramirez.
Ron

December 5, 1967

Dear Joe,

Got in this morning, patrolled all night up north

of the Cua Viet River. Negative enemy contact. Most of my men including myself very tired, very hungry, hit the rack this morning, going out again this evening. Lt Wally may be coming along. Men looked very good last night. Old woman spoiled ambush by walking into it last night.

Ron

P.S. Getting ready to move out again.

December 6, 1967

Dear Joe,

Came in from north patrol this morning tired, cold, and wet. All men in good spirits. Walked about 5,000 meters last night. Set up on hill 5, then 2 ambush positions. Negative results. Lt Wally went with us and let me run the whole patrol. Kleppen ran point and did a fine job. Farmer left on R&R for Oki this morning. After we got in we were given 4 hours sleep then out on patrol south. I took this one out with a CBS cameraman, one CBS reporter, and the Marine CBS liaison man. All the men got a kick out of being on film. We swept out around Vin Ha Phong and netted 2 suspects trying to run from us. Fired over their heads but one got away. Brought them in. CBS Lt treated us all to a beer back in the area and the beer was all out. Gave my men $10 courtesy of CBS—didn't want to take it but he forced it on us. Sleep tonight.

Ron

December 7, 1967

Dear Joey,

Had a good night's sleep last night, feel real good. When we brought the 2 suspects in yesterday, the men cheered us. Something I really think we didn't deserve. (They're only suspects.) The scouts are really beginning to get a good name around here, Lt Wally called us outstanding and said it was a pleasure working with us. I was on my knees praying to God this morning, thanking him for all he has done for the team and asking him for guidance and courage in the weeks ahead. Blessed be the Lord, Jesus Christ—killed one VC tonight. Civilians got in the way. A 7-year-old's foot shot off, a man wounded through the legs, another boy shot up badly, Lord have mercy.

War stinks, it's lousy, I want out, I've had enough. Ron

December 8, 1967

Dear Joe,

Last night was a nightmare. Our patrol ran into 10 men inside a hut. We set up on line then popped a flare. Orders were not to fire until Lt Blair gave the word. Someone fired on the end. Killer team was sent out with me. I ran into the hut to find a man shot through his legs and another lying in the back with his head blown off from the eyes up with his brains hanging out. Another young boy was shot up and his foot was hanging off by a thread. It was a horrible sight. Some of my men cried, "God have mercy, God forgive us!" I bandaged up one man and helped the others. There was blood all over my hands and a dead man right next to me. It seemed a hundred years before the choppers came and took the wounded out. It rained all night and we ended up going back out on patrol. I was numb with despair and disgust.

I hate this damn war. I'm sick and tired of it.
Ron

December 9, 1967

Dear Joe,

Came in yesterday morning and told Lt Ringer I was sick and tired of seeing the dying and killing people and didn't want to take out any more patrols. He told me to think about it and I decided to keep going and if I quit now I'd just be running away from it. Patrol tonight. Lt Wally going along. Good man for the troops. I feel so lousy lately, so disgusted. I wonder sometimes where God is and when he will show me the way. War is such a disgusting, thankless job. My men are all beat. We have been patrolling the past 7 nights straight without a break. 4-5 hours sleep then out again. Man killed last night was a confirmed VC. Major D wants to send my men north to fight the NVA. We are ready. With God we are ready.
Ron

December 10, 1967

In from patrol this morning, no enemy contact. All my men are dead tired. My right foot is all blistered and waterlogged. Rhodes has an infected eye and Pons is sick. Cpl Cozy wants to quit the scouts. I started smoking cigarettes the other day and am now smoking regularly. Lt Wally got us a day's rest. Thank God!!! And we will be going out on a 2-day patrol down south with Lt Blair tomorrow. Received packages from many people. God bless them and God love them. They are what we are fighting for, what we are dying for. Those are the real Americans back there, the ones who really care. God love them. Oh, God bless America. God bless our sacred land. Help me to defend it. God give me strength.

Ron

December 11, 1967

Dear Joe,

Who am I kidding? If I am going to let this war get me down, I'll be nothing better than those punks back in the States telling us to come home. No, I am an American fighting man and by God I'm not going to quit. I'll never quit. I'll die first. War might be hell but the world will be a hell of a place if we don't make a stand now. I know now how Nathan Hale must have felt before he died. I'm proud to be an American, so damn proud. I feel it in my body, in my soul; every part of me is an American and it is red, white and blue all over. We're going to win this war and someday, someway there will be peace. Defending freedom has been our job for almost 200 years. Men have gone before me, brave gallant men have not been afraid to die for freedom. It takes a hellhole like this to show you what being an American is. It's not easy.

Ron

P.S. Big action up north. 2/6 Foxtrot and our men are slugging it out with NVA up north of C-4. Volunteered my men 3 times already, still no go.

December 12, 1967

Dear Joe,

Amtracs and Fox 2/6 combined to kill 65 NVA yesterday in a battle not 3 miles north of us. It was really a slugfest as we took light casualties. Sgt Rick was wounded in the shoulder—he's ok. I was frustrated because my scouts were not allowed to get in the fight and ended up making a patrol to hill 3 down south last night. It was very cold, wet and raining. My men and I were very miserably cold and tired when we got in this morning. It's turning very cold around here lately. Raining all the time. Talked to Major D tonight—going north tomorrow night on patrol.

Ron

December 13, 1967

Dear Joe,

Cpl Cozy and Pons went to Searchlight crew. Cpl Beeson and Sarossy are going up to C-4 for a while to work as radar techs. Rhodes has an infected eye and Farmer is still on R&R. Leaves me with 6 men. Getting two volunteers soon to boost me up to 8 men. Cpl

Beeson procures C-rations for us about every night by way of midnight raids on the supply tent. He steals just about everything he can get his hands on and keeps the team well stocked. We were hit by artillery yesterday afternoon, a few wounded but no one killed.

I took a patrol south yesterday. 12 men held a sweep in front of our lines—checked a few ID cards. Set in on hill 3 for the night. Extremely wet, cold, and miserable night. Most of the men very cold. It is our job, we must do. We will do it.

Ron

December 14, 1967

Dear Joe,

Got in from patrol this morning. Took out 7 men up north, covered around 6,000 meters. It was windy and very cold—by the grace of God it just rained a bit. We left the BN area yesterday afternoon after the chaplain led us in an Our Father (Lord's Prayer). He is a very wonderful man. We caught an ambulance going up to the docks where we caught a Mike "pusher" boat across to the northern side of the Cua Viet River.

I talked to Captain Burger for a while, he is from Newark and quite a friendly officer. We moved out at 1945 and moved up to hill 5 then across to the cemetery then on to the Razorback. Thomas had an accidental discharge with his M-79. The round went straight up and it's a miracle no one was hurt or killed. At around 0100 I moved the men down to a trail near the river, very cold, very windy. Had to keep

moving my fingers, did push-ups to stay alert, came in
at 0545.
Your pal,
Ron

On Being an American
It's not easy to be an American
It takes guts and courage
It takes devotion to our land
It takes love of God, trust in God
It takes sacrifice and suffering to preserve freedom when
it is infringed upon
An American never quits
He is something special
He is modest yet proud
He is the most stainless fighting man the world has ever
known
A true American knows he is an American because he
can feel it in his body
He can feel it in his soul.
When the flag goes by, not just a flag but America passes
by, gallant men pass by, brave men who have given their
lives so we could be free

December 15, 1967
Dear Joe,

   They're playing Christmas music on the radio, "The
First Noel." God, it sounds so wonderful. Times long
since past in years gone by now pass by my eyes. Wonderful warm Christmases; Mom, Dad and all the kids.

Patrol south today. Cpl Beeson and Sarossy picked up a potbelly stove that is now keeping our tent very warm, also dries out our clothing. It is really terrific. Ward came in last night with chow from the mess hall. Last night was a good night, the men's morale is very high now. My best men are LCpl Kleppen now on R&R, PFC Molina, PFC Fant my radioman, and Farmer now on R&R. I have much work to do, so much more to make an outstanding team. Christ Jesus will open the door and lead me. I believe in Jesus Christ. I believe in Mary, mother of God.

Your pal,

Ron

December 16, 1967

Dear Joe,

Got in from patrol this morn. Went to chow. Said hello to Mac. At 1200 we were hit by 150 rounds of enemy artillery. (They just kept coming. I thought they would never stop.) All my men were asleep and ran out of the tent for our bunker. Rounds crashed in again and again, some as close as 6-10 feet away. One blew the tent next to our bunker completely to pieces. There was nothing left. It was hell. I felt we were going to be killed any second. We should have all been killed but God spared us. I ran from the bunker after the arty had lifted in my skivi drawers and a bag of medical bandages. Men were screaming, "Corpman! Corpman!"

I ran to the first hole to find Sgt Botiger blown beyond description. My hands were covered with blood as

I moved to the next hole to find two men decapitated and mangled in a dead heap at the bottom of the hole. Tears came to my eyes, Sgt Bo and I were good friends, he had a wife and a kid he was proud of. I ran across to M.T. where I found another man (Mac) with his arm off and blown beyond description. There was nothing I could do to help them. I felt so helpless. War is such a hell of a thing. I've seen so much damn dying these past 3 months but I've got to keep pushing and hope to live to be 22. Cpl Shartel, my good friend in A Co, was hit in the head, Baret was wounded, many others wounded, at least 7 killed. Sleeping with our boots and clothes on tonight. Our whole tent has shrapnel holes in it.
Ron

December 17, 1967

Dear Joe,

Final total yesterday was 5 men killed, 20 wounded. Most of my men are still a bit shaky. Spent this morning patching up shrapnel holes in the roof of our tent. Mc-Carthy and Sgt Botiger were killed instantly by direct hits. God have mercy on their souls. Went up north today with Kleppen, Molina, and Sgt Hung (our Vietnamese interpreter), found an informer and got info—paid him off. Package from Kathy, God love her.
Ron

December 18, 1967

Dear Joe,

8 men wounded up north of us. Own jets dropped

napalm. A jet blew up and we watched it go down out in the sea north of us. All I saw was smoke. Exum saw it burst into flames. Lord, save the pilot. Early this morning I took my men out for drills and runs—looked fairly good. Lt Hectus, who is now in charge of us, gave me the word to be ready to go in 5 min. Got all the scouts together and took a chopper to the resettlement vill—provided security for the major. Patrol south today, taking 10 men—1 Kit Carson Scout (Ex VC). God protect us all. God help us to do our duty.
Ron

December 19, 1967

Dear Joe,

Got in from patrol this morning. Took new man Evans along for his first patrol. Set up on hill 12 for a few hours then moved down to hill 3. Weather fairly good (no rain). Most of the men are bored with routine south patrols—want to go north or deep south to fight the NVA. Patrol again south today. Farmer back from Okinawa R&R. Marine photog-reporter and Cpl Mangen saw me today about getting some shots of the scouts on patrol. Told me he had heard about us from Cpl Mangen. Will be checking up with him on Thursday. Cpl Beeson very wise, very salty, very poor NCO. Would like to drop him next opportunity I get. 6 days till Christmas. You would never know it. H&S on south patrol also—package from Kathy's father. God bless them all.
Ron

December 20, 1967

Dear Joe,

Got in from south patrol this morning. No enemy contact. My men are looking better each patrol. Lt Hectus asked me if I would like to take a boat trip with a few of my scouts. I said yes and Captain Brunswell, LCpl Kleppen, PFC Molina (wet back), PFC Fant (my radioman), LCpl Farmer (my point man) and I jumped in a 16-foot runabout with a 35 hp engine. Went down the Cua Viet River to My Loc then took the Dam Cho Chua almost 3,500 meters past Vinh Hoa then back again. Captain said I could use the boat in conjunction with river work and patrols. Plan to use it for night patrols up north and night pickups. 5 days till Christmas.

Ron

December 21, 1967

Dear Joe,

All this morning was spent sandbagging and hauling sandbags for the S-2. I jump right in and work with my men. I believe over here everyone must do their share, even a sergeant. I stand at the end of every chow line because I don't believe a sergeant should eat before his troops. I promised I would never cut to the front when I made sergeant. I never have once, nor would I ever. I take great pride in being an NCO and am proud to be a sergeant. I hear people say I am too gung-ho around here. I don't think a Marine can ever be too gung-ho,

no, never too gung-ho. Maybe not gung-ho enough, but never a Marine too gung-ho.
Ron

December 22, 1967

Dear Joe,

Got in from patrol this morning, took out 9 men including the new man, Evans. Most of the team now lives in one tent excluding Cpl Perna and Evans. Thomas has problems and wants to see the chaplain. Rhodes is still up in Dong Ha with an eye infection. We were supposed to sandbag today but SSgt Fisher had to go up north. Wrote letters this evening to many people, thanking them for all the wonderful packages they have sent me. Letters from Mom, Karen, and Uncle Paul (Christmas card), left medical bag at day position yesterday. Yesterday took two men and myself at 0100 on a recon 1,000 meters across the desert to retrieve it. Got it and returned to hill 2. Tired. Will sleep tonight. Cardinal Spellman recently died. God rest his soul.
Ron

December 23, 1967

Dear Joe,

Rhodes came back this morning and I've got my grenadier back. Sgt Ricketts came down to do a story on my Marines. He also plans to take a few movies of the "scouts in action." This afternoon, we ran through a bunch of our drills out in the sand as he shot quite a few feet of us. Cpl Beeson got slapped with a $50 fine

for drinking beer in an unauthorized area (on post).
My new man Evans, the "Hungarian" Sarossy, and Cpl
Beeson were initiated into the scouts, which consisted
of 2 hours of solid hell, harassment and physical ex-
ercise, including burying their heads and rifles in the
sand, blowing bubbles in mud puddles, and rolling in
the mud with their weapons. It ended with all of us
placing black berets on their heads and shaking their
hands.

December 24, 1967

Dear Joe,

Cpl Beeson just got a Christmas package from
home. Christmas record which we are now playing
sounds wonderful. Will be coming in from patrol tomorrow, Christmas morning. Christmas, what a wonderful season, what wonderful memories. Now I'm 21
years old spending my third straight Christmas in a
war 13,000 miles from home on a patrol—ham and C-
rations tonight. Major D says if we contact the enemy to
kill them, 10 men going out. Merry Christmas, peace
on earth, goodwill to all men.
(Someday, I hope.)
Ron

December 25, 1967

Dear Joe,

Just got in from patrol this morning. Merry Christmas, Joe! Negative enemy contact last night, am now
listening to Christmas music on the AFR radio station.

The song is "Comfort and Joy." I guess we're a long way from that. Sgt Ricketts from Marine Corp News came to do a story on the scouts. Can you believe that? One week at CVS, the next they're writing a story on us. God must be working something up there. I feel very good today knowing even though it's Christmas I am serving my country in a war zone 13,000 miles from home. And that is a good feeling. The "Hungarian" Sarossy just pulled out a bottle of wine and we all toasted we might all make it till next Christmas.
Ron

December 26, 1967

Dear Joe,

Worked all day today with my men sandbagging our tent. Farmer and Kleppen went to Dong Ha up the river, it's about an hour's ride and the only means we have of getting to Dong Ha. Read an article written in the Post. I can't understand some of those people back there wanting to quit, wanting to back out just because the war is getting rough. America better get on its feet and wake up before it's too late. This, as far as I'm concerned, is the most important war in our nation's history. If we lose, Communist enslavement of all Asia. If we win, containment of Communism. We are in the greatest crisis our young nation has ever seen. We here, who do the dying and suffering, will not fail. How about those back home?
Ron

December 27, 1967

Dear Joe,

Patrol today, I'll check with the major and find out where I am going. Weather around here for the past week has been blue skies, sunny, not too hot and not too cool. General Westmoreland came to our camp Christmas Day and I was about 10 feet from my Commanding General. I heard Cpl Shartel, who was wounded in the head, was sent home.

Ron

December 28, 1967

Dear Joe,

Took 10 of my men out and made a night landing along the Dam Cho Chua River. We took Vietnamese "junk" boats and had 2 American advisors along. All my men were painted up and wore their black berets as usual. They are very proud of this black hat and look like a real team when they all wear them. After 3 tries at a landing we finally landed 300 meters south of our planned position, then moved along a trail in front of a few huts. Set up an ambush along a trail and laid in ambush for 7 hrs straight. Was hard to stay awake. Had to force myself. Rains came at about midnight. Left ambush at 0300. Flashed light along shoreline and a junk came in to pick us up. Got stuck in sand. Finally got out. Came in wet, cold, tired, miserable as usual. Otherwise, feeling pretty good.

Ron

December 29, 1967

Dear Joe,

Slept in this morning, went to Mass at 1400. Major Donovan told me I would have to provide 6 scouts for a security run to Dia Lock. Took 7 scouts plus myself. Ended up only needing 3 men. Sent the rest of the men back. Took Sarossy (the Hungarian) and the new man, Evans. (Hell of a Marine, hard-charging spirit, may make a good NCO.) Sarossy carried the radio. Ran security for the skimmer boat to Dong Ha. Slept at Dong Ha for the night. Makes our place look like Frontierland. Saw "Return of the Seven"—Marlon Brando. Return to amtracs the following morning.

December 30, 1967

Dear Joe,

Caught a boat to the mouth of the river. A bunch of "new guys" came along. USMC newsman took a picture of Sarossy, Evans, and myself. Did a story on Sarossy. Sometimes it seems there are more newsmen over here than fighting men. Lord! Have the news media done an unforgivable injustice to our effort over here? If they would for once print the true heroism and valor of Americans here rather than blow up isolated punks back home who burn their draft cards. Came back in and found I was going on patrol north tonight. Take care, Joe.

Your pal,

Ron

December 31, 1967

Dear Joe,

New Year's Eve tonight. 1968 has finally come. Came in from north patrol this morning, saw nothing, was a bit cold, not too bad though. SSgt Fisher debriefed me. Really one of the finest Marines I have ever met. I know he will be a success in whatever he does. Major D asked why I hadn't made contact—said I was slipping. Told me if he sent me on patrol up on the DMZ, my men would get some NVA. He said he might send us up to C-4. From what I calculate, I've taken out almost 25 patrols as a sergeant now. Still have a lot to learn. Man came down from press center to do the recordings of all my men for their hometown radio stations.

Ron

January 1, 1968

Dear Joe,

Happy 1968. Held classes in our tent today on first aid and security while on patrol. Many men got drunk last night and raised all kinds of hell, shot off many flares, yelled and screamed. Cpl Beeson and Farmer got very drunk—also Fant. I didn't have a drop and hit the rack early. I think drinking here where we are is very dangerous and if something is not done about it soon, someone is going to be killed. This battalion needs more organization than it has right now. Definitely many men need a good old fashioned #?!# beating. Got my men out playing football (tackle) to toughen them

up and build a great team sprit. Patrol tomorrow night. God bless America. In God we trust.
Ron

January 2, 1968

Dear Joe,

Went on a patrol down south today. At about 0510 Cpl Beeson spotted 3 men observing us from a hill about 300 yds. away. At around 0600 a group of men came down a trail near the hill. I sent Cpl Beeson and Rhodes out to check them out at the same time I walked toward the hill by myself. When I got to the top I was taken under VC automatic weapons fire. I fired back then ran down the hill to regroup my men. My men were quickly on line yelling, swearing, and charging toward the VC under fire. We must have really scared the hell out of them. The men were brave beyond description. Molina is afraid of nothing. We assaulted the hill and the VC fled. Farmer got off a few shots, spotted 4 VC running, I spotted 3.
Ron

January 3, 1968

Dear Joe,

Came in from patrol this morning wet, cold, but feeling real good about making contact with those VC. Men were very brave. They are an outstanding group and we are going to get better. Went on another patrol today. Went with H&S, led them down to Ha Tay Mo where we had yesterday's firefight with the VC. We took

SSgt Hung, our BN interpreter, along and found out from the villagers that 20-25 armed VC were in the village when we made contact. They said the VC ran when we attacked the village. Said VC had green uniforms, submachine guns and rifles. Said no VC were killed in the firefight. Tired, will sleep tonight.
Ron

January 4, 1968

Dear Joe,

Checked out the village of Ha Tay Mo yesterday with our Vietnamese interpreter, SSgt Hung. Ran point for an H&S patrol. Came in around 1600, didn't eat chow. Talked to Cpl Greenleaf for about 30 minutes. He is quite a man with some very good views on religion and life in general. It really amazes me I've kept this diary up so long, Joe. Let me see, 10 more days and it will be 5 months old. I plan to keep writing until I leave in August or until my Vietnam Diary is terminated due to unforeseen causes.
Ron
"John F. Kennedy"—the name radiates courage.

January 5, 1968

Dear Joe,

Got in from north patrol this morning, men walked almost 8,000 meters, weather was cold but no rain, took ex-VC Kit Carson Scout along. He did well. Cpl Beeson and Rhodes, my M-79 man, went up to Dong Ha yesterday and couldn't get back in time for patrol. We set up on the Razorback for a few days. Lately, whenever

I sleep I have "war" dreams, either artillery screaming in or shooting VC. It's on my mind all the time. PFC Molina made LCpl and will be promoted tomorrow. Got into Damar Deltas lines at 0530, slept on the beach until 0700. Skimmer boat picked us up. Ate chow—with Cpl Perna ("Forever Late Perna"). Hit the rack, was awakened at 1000. Patrol south. No slack.
Ron

January 6, 1968

Dear Joe,
    Yesterday started off as a routine patrol—moved into the cemetery off Ha Tay then on to the village of Ha Tay Mo. While I was observing a hill about 300 meters south of our position, I spotted a VC in a green bush hat and green utilities observing us. I came back—called it in on my radio then put my men on line. We moved across on line and pushed 300 or so meters into the village. Our ex-VC scout Sot spotted footprints and the chase was on. Farmer yelled, "They're running away." And we all ran toward the west where I saw a blur in the dark of 6-8 figures. We opened up on them and fired two M-79s—could not tell if we killed any. Men very high spirits. Want to kill VC. Want to fight. A real fighting team. I am very proud.
Ron

January 7, 1968

Dear Joe,
    Had real good sleep last night, feel pretty good. Just

got the word from Lt Wally my men will be going south
today on patrol. Weather yesterday was blue skies and
warm. Monsoons seem to be breaking up again. I'll hold
some immediate action drills this morning. Cpl Beeson
checked the weapons—gave out malaria pills. Quite a bit
of action down south. VC are starting to move around
quite a bit. We plan to stop them. Moved out at 1430.
Lt Wally called us back in to take one of my men to be
used as a guide for B Company on a patrol up north.
Finally left on patrol at 1600.
Ron

January 8, 1968

Dear Joe,

Got in from patrol this morning. Set in out in the
desert west of Vin Ha Phong and Than Hoi trying to
catch any VC moving across at night. ARVN made
contact with a reinforced company of VC south of us,
northwest of us. The ARVN also made contact with
an unestimated number of VC. Farmer, who has only
a few patrols left before he goes home, spotted 2 men
moving west of Than Hoi this afternoon. 2 men from
the H&S patrol hit 2 booby traps on hill 3. Both were
wounded pretty bad. We went out on the amtrac to
bring them in. My scouts acted as security. Had to leave
Molina and Sarossy out in the driving rain to replace
the 2 men hit. VC getting very active now down south
of us. It's going to be a hot spring.
Ron

January 9, 1968

Dear Joe,

Got up this morning and got the word. Patrol south. Lt Hectus, who is in charge of me and the rest of my scouts, took 4 of us as security when we brought a young Vietnamese girl to her village after a few Marines on our lines caught her selling marijuana cigarettes. Patrol is a short one to hill 2. I'm sure quite a few VC are moving south of our lines and we must attack them now.

January 10, 1968

Dear Joe,

Came in from patrol this morning. Sarossy found a VC booby trap marker and brought it in. Sent Cpl Beeson, Molina, and Sarossy to Dong Ha on a security run. Tomorrow we will be going on a boat to the village of Dy Lock to protect the MEDCAP team—no patrol tonight. Ron

January 11, 1968

Dear Joe,

Today my scouts and myself went to Dy Lock (which is about 2 miles down the river). Captain Brunswell, who is in charge of civil affairs, ran a MEDCAP for the people of this village. Lord, you should have seen some of these people. Some with infections and rashes all over their body. Babies crying, sometimes I wonder if these people know what a bar of soap is. Kids crawl all over you, ask for cigarettes or anything else they can get

off you. Today after seeing these people, I just know we
have to not only secure their freedom but must also
help them out.

Came back from MEDCAP (by skimmer boat),
landed at Cua Viet. Got chow for my men then Lt Hectus told us we were going out on patrol. Most men tired
and angry. What do they want, they asked to be scouts.
Besides, we're Marines.
Ron

                                        January 12, 1968
Dear Joe,

Got the word 2 companies of VC are down in the
area of Hay Tay Mo. 3 patrols out last night hooked up,
then my scouts led Major Burger to the patrols at 0530
this morning. I took my men to the west of Hay Tay Mo
while the major's men swept south through the village.
All they found was a few fighting holes and a Viet Cong
cartridge belt. My men spotted 2 men running from
us. We opened fire over their heads but they continued to run. We then aimed in and fired. As they got
away we spotted another group of 15 running south.
We chased them for a few hundred meters but our flak
jackets knocked us out. Fant, my radioman, almost had
heat exhaustion. Came in, hit the rack.
Ron

                                        January 13, 1968
Dear Joe,

Major Donovan sent us on a routine patrol south

this morning and we ended up finding 7 booby traps near hill 3 area. I disarmed 3 and Farmer got the other 2. We blew 2 more in place. The one I almost stepped on was made of a large steel illumination round casing filled with C-4. The others were made of tin cans full of C-4 explosive with fisherman's wire used for trip wire. I played real close to death today disengaging the traps, but my faith in God gave me all the strength. I said, "Lord, you can have me if you want but I'd appreciate living just a bit longer to help save some souls and my country." We brought the booby traps back plus VC booby trap markers. Major D was very pleased. Taking my men deep north tonight. Morale is high.
Ron

January 14, 1968

Dear Joe,

Patrol north last night up around hill 2 which is a few hundred meters northwest of the lake. The night was clear and the moon very bright. We walked almost 9,000 meters total and the men were a bit tired. Observation from hill 2 was excellent although we made no contact or saw any enemy. This was Farmer's last patrol and he should be heading home in another 2 weeks or so.

Kleppen extended for 6 more months and will go home for 30 days, then come back in March. Slept in this morning and got the word we would finally get a night off. At about 1900 Reaction was called out and my men went to help a patrol which had spotted an

estimated 25-30 VC down south. It was one hell of a mess and confusion and I was glad when it was all over.
Ron

                                    January 15, 1968
Dear Joe,
    Got in from Reaction patrol at 0100 last night and woke up at 0900 this morning. Got my men up at 1030. Lt Hectus said no patrol and I gave the men the morning to clean their gear. This afternoon I had the men play tackle football and Farmer, Kleppen, Rhodes and myself beat Molina, Cpl Perna, Cpl Beeson and Fant 30-12 in a hard-fought game in the sand. After the game I told the men to be out back for squad tactics in 10 minutes. Cpl Beeson blew up and we had a loud argument about giving the men a rest. I told him practice makes perfect and this is the way it would be and if he didn't like it I'd drop him from the squad. He was very bitter. Men are a very tight group. Beeson is my only pain. May get rid of him.
Ron

                                    January 16, 1968
Dear Joe,
    Patrol north tonight. Will catch a boat across the river around 1900 tonight then move out around 2000. Will be patrolling up north of the lake. I brought Cpl Beeson up in front of Lt Hectus today and the Lt said the next time Beeson was insubordinate he would go up in front of the colonel. I ask God for his help and

that he might help Beeson. (He's just a 19-year-old kid who acts like he's 16.)

Ron

P.S. Found out today Beeson had saved a man back in the States and was put up for a medal.

January 17, 1968

Dear Joe,

Came in from north patrol this morning, saw nothing. Took Cpl Bare (the ex-DI) plus 2 other H&S men along with the team. Cpl Perna thinks he has a hernia. PFC Sarossy is sick with a bad case of diarrhea and Farmer has about 2 weeks left so I'm not sending him out anymore. This left me with 7 hard-charging scouts. Perna should be better soon and Sarossy is feeling good also. Scouts keep us very busy, usually there isn't much time for anything. All my men are close to God. Sarossy, whose family escaped from Hungary in '56, is very religious and Molina (Rudy the wet back) prays the rosary as I do also. Cpl Beeson was called into the company office today to find out he had been put up for the Navy Commendation Medal for saving a man's life back in the States. People sure are strange. They will fool you every time.

Ron

January 18, 1968

Dear Joe,

Second day straight and no patrol—really can't believe all the slack we're getting. Read a book, "The Best

Loved Poems of the American People," and it's an inspiring book. We sandbagged most of our tent today
and I can truthfully say our tent is one of the cleanest
and best looking in the battalion. Molina got a package
today—we eat! Haven't had much mail lately but know
everyone is fine. Time is going fast in a way, while in
other ways it seems I've been here 100 years. I love my
great nation and am ready to die for freedom.
Ron

"Fear not that ye have died for naught.
The torch ye threw to us we caught.
Ten million hands will hold it high,
And Freedom's light shall never die!
We've learned the lessons that ye taught
In Flanders Fields."
—R.W. Lillard, Best Loved Poems of the American People

January 19, 1968
Dear Joe,
    1/3 patrol made heavy contact with the NVA north
of us this morning. They (grunts) said the patrol walked
into a horseshoe ambush. One Lt was brought in dead.
Shot through the head. The chaplain said a prayer as I
knelt by also. Most of the others weren't wounded too
bad. I don't know why it didn't bother me much seeing
death today. Most of all I was angry and told Farmer
they (NVA) would pay! I swore they would pay. Most
of my men were very angry we couldn't go up and get
in the fight. I must have volunteered them 5 times, to

be turned down every time. There are two types of Marines in this battalion, those that sit on their rear ends (they talk the most and give the most advice) and the fighting Marines (we do the fighting, patrolling and dying) who don't say too much.

Ron

Monday, January 22, 1968

Father R. Harrington
Hospital Chaplain
Danang, Vietnam

Dear Mr. and Mrs. Kovic,

As you know, Ronald is a patient at our hospital in Danang. I imagine that the Navy Department has informed you about the extent of his injuries. Tonight he is doing well and seems to be comfortable and in excellent spirits. His injury is serious but he has great will power and tremendous determination. His faith and fortitude will see him through. Your son is one of the finest men I have ever met. You can certainly be extremely proud of him. He sends his regards to his brothers and sisters. If I can be of any assistance, please let me know.

Sincerely,
Father R. Harrington
Hospital Chaplain
Danang, Vietnam

July 26, 1968
Massapequa, NY

Dear Joe,

On 20 Jan, 1968 in a firefight north of the Cua Viet River, Sarossy was killed and 3 other of my men wounded. I was shot through the foot and then through the right shoulder, which paralyzed me when it severed my spinal cord. I've been in 4 different hospitals in the past 6 months. I received Last Rights in Danang but God spared me. The doctors say I will never walk again and will have to live in a wheelchair for the remainder of my life.

May I say that through these 6 months I've never lost faith in myself, my God, or my country. I believe in everything I wrote in this diary with all my heart and soul. I now, Ronald Lawrence Kovic, being of sound mind and body, end this Vietnam Diary in my home where it all began. Began July 7, 1967, completed July 26, 1968.

Ronald Lawrence Kovic

PART II

BREAKING THE SILENCE OF THE NIGHT

A time comes when silence is betrayal.
—Martin Luther King Jr.

A VIOLENT SPRING

February 1969

I t was a violent spring. Martin Luther King Jr. had been killed in Memphis and I had just begun reading Senator Robert F. Kennedy's book *To Seek a Newer World* at the Bronx VA hospital when Kennedy was assassinated on June 6, 1968, at the Ambassador Hotel in Los Angeles. He had been the antiwar candidate and I remember picking up his book with hesitation at first, his views seeming so very different from my own, but there was something that drew me toward him and his call to end the war that spring. Maybe it was the wounded all around me on the paraplegic ward or the hundreds of Americans who continued to die each week. I was deeply saddened when he died, just as I had been when his brother, President John F. Kennedy, was killed in Dallas in 1963.

I had been so certain of victory, but I now began to realize more and more that we were not going to win in Vietnam, and that realization was painful and devastating. I felt betrayed and could not understand why my government had not done all that it could to win

the war. Did they have any idea how much we had sac-
rificed; how many had already died and been maimed
like myself? I was sad and depressed and would often go
down to the hospital library on the first floor where I
would read for hours at a time trying to forget the war.

The next book that I read was about the life of Vice
President Hubert Humphrey, and I remembered listening to his voice on the Armed Forces Radio during my
second tour of duty and writing in my diary how much
hearing him and his determination to stay the course
and not give up in Vietnam had inspired me.

Several days later I discovered the diary of Che Gue-
vara, the Cuban revolutionary who had gone to Bolivia
and was later killed there while attempting to inspire a
revolution. I felt uneasy at first holding the book in my
hands as I sat in my wheelchair, afraid that someone
might come up to me and catch me reading about the
"enemy," but I now wanted to know who this enemy
was, who were these people I had been taught to hate
and sent to fight and kill.

I remembered watching the 1968 Democratic Na-
tional Convention in Chicago on TV at the VA hospital
with other paralyzed veterans in their wheelchairs, the
crowds in the streets outside the convention hall chanting, "The whole world is watching! The whole world is
watching!" as antiwar demonstrators were beaten and
bloodied by police and dragged into waiting paddy
wagons.

Most of my fellow veterans were angry at the protest-
ers, cursing them and calling them traitors, but I felt

very differently that night. What the police had done was wrong, and for the first time, though I did not share it with anyone yet, I began to sympathize with the demonstrators.

It was not long after that that I left the hospital and began attending classes at Hofstra University on Long Island, determined to rise above what had happened to me and begin a new life after the war. Inspired by President Kennedy's call to service, I hoped to study political science and be elected to office someday. It was a quiet and peaceful campus, so different from Vietnam and the hospital, and it was at the university that I began to hear the passionate exchange of ideas and different points of view. Many of the discussions had to do with the war and why it had to end. There were the lit candles and the moratoriums, the John Lennon song "Give Peace a Chance," and I listened to the Woodstock album and Jimi Hendrix's wild rendition of "The Star-Spangled Banner" for the first time.

There was the infamous My Lai massacre poster, *And babies?* It was shocking and I could not help but think back to that night during my second tour of duty when we shot those women and children by mistake, all those bloody bodies, the old man with his brains hanging out and that Vietnamese child whose foot had nearly been shot off, dangling by a thread. I continued to attend classes, still keeping my thoughts and feelings about the war deep inside of me and sharing them with no one. It was during this period that I read Henry

David Thoreau's essay "Civil Disobedience" and was immediately struck by the concept of resistance to civil government and noncooperation with evil, which seemed to directly contradict what I had believed as a boy: that my country was always right and could do no wrong. The whole idea that we as citizens had a right to follow our conscience and resist laws that were unjust and immoral had a powerful effect on me.

I was later to learn that Senator Joseph McCarthy had attempted to ban Thoreau's essay and that Mahatma Gandhi and Martin Luther King's philosophy of creative nonviolence as a tactic for social change had been strongly influenced by their reading of "Civil Disobedience." There was *The Autobiography of Malcolm X* and *Nigger*, a book by Dick Gregory, and Joseph Conrad's *Heart of Darkness*, which exposed the brutality and horror of colonialism. I read Jerry Rubin's *Do It!* and Abbie Hoffman's *Revolution for the Hell of It*, astounded at the sheer audacity of these two "Yippie" radicals and their willingness to stand up to the most powerful government in the world and its policy in Vietnam. They were wild and outrageous and believed in revolution and were not afraid to say it or write about it and act it out.

There was the article in *Ramparts* magazine by Army Green Beret Sergeant Donald Duncan, who had turned against the war, and I recall someone from the university mentioning that a Vietnam veteran from Suffolk County Community College on Long Island was now heading the SDS (Students for a Democratic

Society) on his campus. There were the Columbia University sit-ins and the alternative New York City radio station WBAI, which I listened to in my room late at night, deeply moved by talk of protest and revolution, power to the people, and provocative antiwar songs that brought tears to my eyes, giving me an entirely different perspective on what was happening in Vietnam and here at home.

Many of the students had become so angry and frustrated with the war and what was going on that they had begun to give up on America. Many wondered if we were ever really a "democracy" to begin with, while still others spoke openly about leaving the country and abandoning America forever. I was still trying to be a good student, but I could not help but be affected by all the things that were happening around me. One day while sitting in the back of a crowded auditorium, I listened to the words of Congressman Allard Lowenstein, who had come to our campus fiercely condemning the war and telling us all to not give up, that it was "better to reclaim the country than abandon it!"

One afternoon I received a call from my friend Bobby Muller, whom I had first met at the Bronx VA hospital only a few months before and who had also been paralyzed in Vietnam, asking me if I would join him at Levittown Memorial High School on Long Island later that week to speak against the war. I was hesitant at first, telling him I wasn't sure. I had never spoken in public before and the thought of giving a speech against the war frightened me.

When I got off the phone, I felt an uncomfortable burning in my stomach. A part of me wanted to speak for all I had seen in Vietnam and the hospital and for all the thoughts and feelings I'd been having while attending classes at the university; and another part could not help but think of what might happen to me if I did. I was afraid. Would I end up in some FBI file, no longer the quiet student sitting in his wheelchair alone on the outskirts of the demonstrations but now a direct participant, a radical? I would be stepping over the line and joining with the very people I had once thought of as traitors. What would my mother and father think if they found out? And the veterans at the university—what would they say? Would they feel I had betrayed them?

Bobby called me several times that week, sounding a bit impatient, but again I hesitated, telling him that I hadn't made up my mind yet. One night I asked him if he would call me the following morning, which was the day of the speech, saying I would let him know for sure. I could hardly sleep that night, tossing and turning, tormented by fear and doubt, trapped between the awful twilight of what might happen to me if I did speak and what I knew would continue to happen if I remained silent.

BREAKING THE SILENCE

And some of us who have already begun
to break the silence of the night have
found that the calling to speak is often a
vocation of agony, but we must speak.
—Martin Luther King Jr.

When the phone rang early the next morning, I picked it up half-asleep and told Bobby that I had decided to join him that day. This was more than fifty years ago but I still remember driving down to the high school in my hand-controlled car thinking of all the things I wanted to say to the students. I parked, transferred into my wheelchair, and pushed over to the entrance of the school and into the auditorium. Bobby was already sitting on the stage in his wheelchair talking to one of the teachers. I was then carried up a few steps, where I joined him. I turned my head and looked out at all the young people in the audience, thinking how much they reminded me of myself only a few years before, so young and innocent, so trusting and willing to believe without question.

Bobby spoke first and a few minutes later it was my turn. I approached the microphone slowly, pushing my wheelchair to the very center of the stage, and started to talk. I told them about the VA hospital—the overcrowded conditions, the rats on the ward—and just as I began to speak about how I had been shot and paralyzed in Vietnam, the fire bell rang. The auditorium quickly cleared out, one of the teachers telling us that someone had just called in a bomb threat. I didn't know what to think at first. I was frightened, angry, and outraged, all at the same time. Why would anyone want to stop me from speaking? Who could that voice on the other end of the phone have been? Was it another student, a teacher, an angry parent? What could they have possibly been thinking? I would never know for sure, only that someone had made an effort to stop me from speaking that day, and that affected me deeply.

We all went outside and after a brief discussion decided to head over to the high school football field where we assembled the students in the grandstand and I continued speaking, more determined than ever to not be silenced.

In the months and years to follow, there would be Kent State and my first demonstration against the war in Washington, DC, the VVAW (Vietnam Veterans Against the War), arrests, tapped phones, undercover agents, and many more speeches, as my political awakening continued and I began to discover an America far different than the one I had once believed in. There were the trials and days and nights I spent in jail in my wheelchair, feeling more like a criminal than someone who had risked his life for his cosuntry, but I continued to speak. Perhaps it was survivor's guilt, or my own desperate need to be forgiven and keep others from having to come back like me, but as I sat before those crowds I began to open up my heart in a way that I had never done before, sharing everything, all the horrors and nightmares, all the things I had locked deep inside of myself and had for so long been afraid to say.

In many ways I was confessing the sins of America. Yet in all the speeches I gave that spring, I never once mentioned that night of October 15, 1967, when I had accidently shot and killed one of my own men. That secret was still buried deep within me.

There were many nights driving home to my apartment after those speeches feeling exhausted and deeply troubled, unable to sleep, knowing that if I did, the nightmares would return and I would be back in Vietnam all over again, only to awaken a few hours later with my heart pounding in my chest, feeling terribly alone and wondering why I was putting myself through all this pain and agony.

KENNEDY

It had only been a few years before when I had sat in the living room of my house in Massapequa, Long Island, with tears in my eyes listening to President John F. Kennedy call my generation to "a new frontier," urging us all to be ready to "pay any price, bear any burden, meet any hardship, support any friend, oppose any foe to assure the survival and success of liberty." But those words seemed hollow to me now. Somewhere along the way we had taken a wrong turn, somewhere through it all America had veered tragically off course, leaving behind its sacred ideals and betraying the very roots of its revolutionary past. Instead of a great champion of liberty, America had emerged an impostor, a fraud, a dangerous, corrupt, frightening monstrosity. America had lived a terrible lie. We had been on the wrong side of history. The great defender of liberty had become the tyrant, the bully, the cruel exploiter of "your tired, your poor, your huddled masses yearning to breathe free."

Wearing the deceitful mask of the great liberator and promising freedom and democracy, we had robbed and raped, blackmailed, murdered, and perverted our way around the world, supporting the most despicable despots as we expanded our bloody empire, causing the death and suffering of countless human beings. I now understood what Martin Luther King Jr. had meant when he had called America "the greatest purveyor of violence in the world today: my own government."

My reading continued with *The State and Revolution* by Vladimir Lenin and *Poems from the Prison Diary of Ho Chi Minh.* There was George Jackson's *Prison Letters* and a powerful book by Felix Greene called *The Enemy: What Every American Should Know about Imperialism.* There was the documentary film *Hearts and Minds* and the agonizing scene of the grief-stricken Vietnamese woman being held back by family members as she tried to crawl into the grave of her husband who had just been killed in an American air strike; and the haunting scene of a Vietnamese child screaming and running naked from her village after being severely burned in a napalm attack.

The war raged on and my speeches grew angry and bitter at a government I couldn't trust anymore.

With the passage of time, I found purpose in my anger by the writing and publication of my first book, *Born on the Fourth of July.* I continued to protest for the rights of disabled veterans, culminating in the sit-in and hunger strike I led in 1974 demanding better treatment for America's veterans. I later wrote about this in my book *Hurricane Street.* While I achieved some literary success and was able to gain ground for the rights of my fellow veterans, my own personal demons continued to haunt me, tearing at my soul. It would be over a decade before I would finally be able to face them.

EXPATRIATE

*If you are lucky enough to have lived in
Paris as a young man, then wherever you
go for the rest of your life it stays with
you, for Paris is a moveable feast.*
—Ernest Hemingway, to a friend, 1950

I n late December of 1981, I was returning to my
country with a new goal in mind, a goal so terribly
ambitious that it seemed to tower above all my previous feelings of failure and defeat.

The Concorde began to descend through the thick
winter clouds and I could now see the great mass of water called the Long Island Sound below and the island
that I had grown up on as a boy. I was so happy to be
home and my heart literally sang as I strained to lift
my paralyzed body up from my seat. When we touched
down, the loneliness of all the months I had spent in
Europe trying to be an expatriate returned and I began
to cry.

As we headed toward the arrival gate, all the people
and places that had once meant so much to me came

flooding back: my mother and father, the old neighborhood, our house on Toronto Avenue, and all my
friends. It had only been months before that I had literally cursed out the land of my birth, determined to
leave America forever. Just before departing in August
1981, I had written a bitter poem called "The Rugged
Individualist," where I raged against the government
and those who had sent me to Vietnam. I was fed up
with America, tired of being harassed and hounded by
the police for my antiwar views, beaten and arrested,
my phone tapped, plagued by nightmares and anxiety
attacks. As far as I was concerned, the government was
the enemy and America had become a dangerous country that I now hated and feared.

I had thought of all the great writers and poets who'd
fled the country to become expatriates—Hemingway,
Fitzgerald, Gertrude Stein—I would be just like them.
Perhaps I would meet a beautiful woman in Paris. I
imagined us living together. We might even adopt a
child and begin a new life far from Vietnam and the
madness back home. There was, of course, a deeper
reason for my departure, though I kept it well hidden,
rarely allowing it to surface.

For nearly three months I had wandered through
Europe searching for a home—Paris, Amsterdam, Dub-
lin, Florence, then back to Paris, where I met the French
philosopher and political activist Jacques Monet and
his wife, the gifted sculptor Maria Benoit, who had
been first introduced to me at a book party in New
York City just before I left the country. Jacques, who

had recently taken a leave of absence from his position at the Sorbonne University, immediately invited me to his spacious town house on the rue de Rivoli, explaining that he and Maria would be away on a lecture tour of the United States for several weeks and that I was welcome to stay at their place for as long as I wished. "Make yourself at home, brother!" Jacques said. "You can have my bedroom and my maid Cassandra will look after you while I'm away. My sixteen-year-old son Albert will also be sharing the house with you."

I was soon to discover that Albert, as philosophical and eccentric as his father, was having a wild affair with a woman twice his age. Rather than being repulsed by the fling, his father seemed pleased. "How is a young man supposed to learn?" Jacques once said to me. "This is Paris, Ronald. We are sexually free here in ways most Americans cannot begin to imagine."

> *The language of sex had yet to be invented.*
> *The language of the senses was yet to be explored.*
> —Anaïs Nin, *Delta of Venus*

As I slowly settled into my new surroundings, I began to feel more and more at ease. Perhaps Paris would be the answer, and as I lay in Jacques Monet's bed each night listening to the moans and groans of Albert and his lover, I started to draw in my diary crude pictures of men with enormous penises bulging in the American night, with giant vaginas spread wide open waiting for deliverance. My physical and sexual loss in Vietnam had been a devastating blow, and as I listened to Albert and his lover, I wondered if sexual intimacy might still be possible in my life despite my horrific wound.

I was still in my thirties with the same lustful yearnings that most young men of that age have, but Vietnam had violently ended all that. Was sex for me, as Anaïs Nin had said, in need of a new language, a new definition? Could I, despite my cataclysmic loss, begin to explore that new language?

As young Albert and his lover kept moaning and groaning each night, I continued my erotic drawings, followed by some moans and groans of my own as I pulled and twisted the one nipple I could still feel, until I was about to explode. I remember thinking that if my mother ever discovered my erotic drawings she would surely call them obscene and insist that I immediately go to confession. But there in Jacques's town house, rather than feeling guilty, I felt free.

Paris soon became an adventure, or a "moveable feast" in Hemingway's words, and I began to meet more artists and expatriates like myself. Before I left the States, I'd been given the number for Jim Haynes, an American expatriate, or "citizen of the world" as he preferred to be called, who held dinner parties and salons every Sunday night at his loft. It was there that I hoped I might meet some new friends and perhaps a woman I could become involved with.

On one particular Sunday night it was Jim, I believe,

out of the kindness of his heart for the lost soul that I was back then, who invited me to a party the following week at the loft of Pablo Picasso's daughter Paloma. Upon my arrival, I was carried up six steep flights of stairs by several friendly partygoers. It was a beautiful home and as I wheeled into the living room, I immediately noticed her father's painting *Flower in Hands*. My first thought was, *Is this the original? Is it safe up there and is Paloma concerned that someone might try and steal it?*

At the end of the night, two extremely inebriated Frenchmen carried me down the stairs. I don't know how we ever made it to the street below, but I hugged both of them, grateful for their help. "What a party!" I remember shouting as one of them hailed a cab and gently lifted me into the backseat.

Feeling every bit French and wearing my bright blue beret and red scarf each morning, I would push my wheelchair down the rue de Rivoli and often find myself sitting at my favorite café across from the Hotel Regina. I would order croissants and their espresso that was so strong it would make my heart skip a beat. After breakfast I would wheel past the Louvre thinking of all the great artists and their paintings, then push myself across a bridge over the river Seine where I would pause in the middle and stare off into the distance at the Eiffel Tower.

One particularly sunny afternoon as I sat in the café and watched an American tourist bus pull up across the street, I remember thinking how isolated and out of touch my countrymen seemed in this foreign culture. *I'm not an American anymore!* I thought bitterly. *I'm not a part of you.* Yet in the back of my mind I was confused. Here were people getting off the bus who looked like my friends and neighbors from Massapequa—and just as that thought crossed my mind, my anger and resentment seemed to fade, and I began to feel a love and genuine concern for them. They were Americans, citizens of the country I had abandoned, and just as a part of me did not want to have anything to do with them ever again, another part knew we would forever be connected.

The weeks passed and autumn came to Paris. I thought of Hemingway and how he had traveled there in the 1920s with dreams like myself of becoming a great writer. It soon grew crisp and cold and the rains came to Paris and ice began to form on the puddles in the streets. Jacques's maid Cassandra would greet me every morning with a hot cup of espresso, a delicious croissant, and a friendly *"Bonjour, mon ami!"*

It was in Jacques's apartment that I finally opened up my bag of writings: hundreds of pages of a novel that I had been struggling with ever since the publication of *Born on the Fourth of July* in 1976. Written in one month, three weeks, and two days in the fall of 1974 on the dining room table of my apartment in Santa Monica, California, *Born on the Fourth of July* had received a rave review on the front page of the Sunday *New York Times Book Review*, C.D.B. Bryan calling it "the most personal and honest testament published thus far by any young man who fought in the Vietnam War." For a kid who had barely made it out of high school and had to go to summer school in order to graduate, that remarkable review had given me a confidence I sorely lacked. Yet, despite the success of my book, something seemed to still be missing, something deep inside that had not yet been said, something desperately crying to come out. Perhaps this new book would be the answer.

As I sat behind my typewriter at Jacques's dining room table, it all came pouring out, almost as if I had been waiting to write those words ever since I'd come home from the war. Late one night I scribbled in my diary,

> I am hoping and praying that the truth will set me free, save me from this awful torment. It does not matter how short the sentences are, the structure or style of my writing. In moments like these none of that matters. It simply is a confession, a scream. I am calm. I am centered and completely at peace. I have come home to my most true and authentic self. It is the truth I now write from the deepest parts of my being, from the most sacred parts of my humanity.

I continued to write through the night as if no time had passed. I was exhausted and my back ached, but none of that seemed to matter. I felt wonderful, tired, but completely consumed by my writing. I would drink a couple cups of coffee, and with a new surge of energy work for another hour or so as the bright lights of the morning began to fill the room. I would then neatly stack all the pages next to my typewriter, head into Jacques's bedroom, and transfer out of my wheelchair and into his bed.

As I lay there one morning, I started to believe that there just might be a way out of this thing, that there could still be redemption in all that had happened, all that I had gone through. This great book which had been growing in my mind would become my way out, my shield against everything that threatened to intimidate and overwhelm me. I would write a Great American Novel and it would be unlike any book that had ever been written before. I was feeling stronger and more confident. I would no longer be afraid. I would no longer run and hide. Even with all the shame and guilt from what had happened in Vietnam, I felt exhilarated. Something told me that as long as I was committed to this great endeavor, nothing could harm me: not the government, not the police, not even the ghost of the man I had killed in the war that still haunted me.

Wilson and the children were dead, and though I knew I could never bring them back, perhaps this "great American confession" might be a way to assuage the guilt that had for so long tormented my soul. I made an important decision in Jacques's apartment and that decision had strengthened me. It was a crazy thought but maybe this novel could be the answer. Perhaps the writing of this book could be my redemption.

In my diary I wrote,

I will hide no longer; I will use this Great American Novel to allow me passage into that dark and foreboding night. These words will be my protector, my shield, they will guide me on my journey; for there is safety in the language of the dead, there is comfort in this darkness that shall never end.

RETURN TO AMERICA

December 1981

I was returning to America with a new goal in mind, a goal so terribly ambitious that it seemed to rise above all my past feelings of failure and defeat. I placed all the writing and scraps of notes written on napkins in Paris cafés into my traveling bag, determined to continue the book upon my return to the United States.

The first thing I saw after getting off the plane, on my way to baggage claim, was a huge Christmas tree in the main hall decorated with colorful ornaments and flags from all the countries of the world. Next to the tree were children singing Christmas carols. They had come down that day to JFK International Airport and I could not help but feel as if they were singing to me and welcoming me home after a return from my exile. I thought of going out to Massapequa and visiting my mom and dad, but the frigid New York temperatures made me want to get back to California as soon as possible.

I spent the night at one of the airport motels and

the following morning got on a plane headed west, flying over that great American continent I had crossed
for the first time as a young marine nearly fifteen years
before. As I settled back in my seat, I pulled out my
address book that had been zipped up in one of the
pouches of my traveling bag and thumbed through
it, thinking about all my friends in LA. I got excited
imagining the warm Southern California weather, the
beautiful Pacific Ocean, and all the possibilities of love,
romance, and adventure that the West Coast always
seemed to offer.

THE SEA LODGE

I t is early 1982 and I am in my room at the Sea Lodge in Venice, California, several blocks up from the beach. I lie on my bed staring out the sliding glass window of my third-floor room and down into the parking lot of the Baja Cantina. It is sometime in the late afternoon and I have been writing all day. I write with a terrible fury, as if I cannot get the words down fast enough, as if each second matters and if I don't hurry up I might suddenly die before I'm able to say all I have to say.

I am completely and totally dedicated to my project. It is all I do, with the exception of taking breaks for lunch and dinner and occasional strolls along the Ocean Front Walk in my wheelchair. When I'm not writing or talking into my tape recorder here on my bed at the Sea Lodge, I am reading aloud to my friend Pat. Sometimes my voice grows horse and Pat pleads for me to stop: "Ronnie, you've got to rest. Let's get out of here for a while. You've got to take a break!" Sometimes it takes hours for me to come down from all the intense work I'm doing.

I don't remember ever working harder in my life. And it goes on like this for months, seven days a week, fourteen, sixteen hours a day. The manuscript keeps growing, it's almost three feet high by mid-April, driven by something I can only now begin to understand.

The Sea Lodge is where I can finally put all these pieces together, all these scraps of notes that I have saved, every word that I have written in all the hotel and motel rooms, all these hundreds of manuscript pages stuffed into that traveling bag, always running from myself, the anxiety attacks, the nightmares, the speeding cabs and roaring jets in half a dozen American cities, all over Europe and in Jacques's apartment in Paris, and even on the Concorde on the way back to the States. I am determined to overcome, to rise above everything I've been through—and whatever the cost, I feel it is worth it, a chance to redeem myself, a stream of consciousness, an uninterrupted thousand-page monologue speaking to the man I killed in the war.

It is very difficult writing the opening section. The words do not come easily. I feel my pulse quicken, my heart beating faster and faster. There is still a part of me resisting writing this material, a voice screaming inside of me to stop, yet I decide to continue on, determined to complete the book.

October 15, 1967. That is the night that it happened, a night that I will never forget, a night that will haunt me for as long as I live. I was twenty-one and you were nineteen. I was your sergeant, your squad leader, the man who was supposed to lead you, to protect you. I was responsible for your life and all the other lives in the platoon, but I failed you that night. I failed you and nothing on earth, no God, no prayer or plea, no matter how beseeching, will ever bring you back.

The entire novel, titled *An American Elegy*, will be set in the graveyard of the marine I killed in Vietnam. Like James Joyce's *Ulysses*, it will all occur in one afternoon—but it will be my confession, the story of what happened that night and all the years that followed . . .

I think of Thomas Gray's "Elegy Written in a Country Churchyard," a poem sent to me anonymously not long after I returned home from Vietnam, leaving me shaken. Who could have sent that poem—one of the men from my platoon, someone from Georgia who attended your funeral? Your mother, your father? Who would do such a thing, and why?

I think about how your mother and father must still come to stand before your grave, their son, their boy, killed in Vietnam at nineteen. Do they know I was the one who killed you, that I was the one who pulled the trigger that night? They must know by now. I'm sure they know. They have probably known all these years, but still they say nothing?

Am I crazy? How much more am I going to let myself suffer? Am I robbing from the crypt? Am I stealing from the dead? When will I stop exploiting your death? When will I decide to live in the here and now? When will I let you rest?

Am I doing what I have heard others sometimes do when they visit the site of the deceased, speaking to the dead as if they are still alive and can hear what is being said? Ever since I came home from the war, I've had a recurring nightmare that I visit the graveyard where you are buried. In every nightmare I sit before your grave pleading with you to forgive me. *I'm sorry, I'm so sorry*, I say, tears streaming down my face, begging for your forgiveness, telling you that I made a terrible mistake and that in a moment of panic and doubt I mistook you for the enemy.

That night keeps coming back. I cannot forget what happened. It pursues me and haunts me, that terrible night. I ran from your death deeply ashamed at what I had done. There is so much guilt, so much pain. I hide behind anything that will keep you and that night away from me, but you will not leave me; even in death you follow me wherever I go.

Sometimes I hear your voice screaming inside of me; my chest tightens and it becomes difficult to breathe. Even writing it down on paper or talking it into the tape recorder is a stressful and frightening experience.

A SIMPLE TALK IN A COUNTRY GRAVEYARD

It will be nothing more than a simple talk in a country graveyard, a moment of reckoning of sorts, shared between life and death. I want to tell you of that night, and of what happened in all those years you would have lived if I hadn't killed you; a very private conversation on this dark and rainy afternoon, a quiet time together that no one else will share but you and me.

A great bird flutters over the graveyard, as black as pitch, as dark as night. It is raining and there is no wind, there is only this gravestone and memory of you, and I ask you to listen to me now, even in death. Please, I can't wait any longer, the death tide has come; the time has come to speak. I can barely remember your face. I met with you for only a minute. It was in the battalion area just before we were about to leave on patrol. I can hardly remember what you said. You told me you had a wife. I think you said that. You were from Georgia—Dalton, Georgia. I asked how old you were. I don't remember anything else. The darkness came and it was time to leave on patrol. You had a mustache with the ends curled up in wax. We did not talk after that. I would not hear your voice again until you were dying and choking in the ditch later that night.

Many times I imagine riding a motorcycle at high speed, aware that at any second I might be thrown off and killed, yet I keep pressing the throttle down harder and harder, challenging myself to go deeper into my trauma, knowing that if I am able to complete this book it might just free me from these terrible feelings of guilt and shame.

I had often thought of what it would be like to kill a man, how it would feel to pull the trigger and take a life out of this world, to blow away another human being, to blow away a gook. *I'll do it*, I thought. *If I have to, I'll do it.*

I can still remember the moment it happened. It was raining and we were walking on patrol just south of the battalion area. It was sometime around 2300 when we crossed onto the edge of the village. It was then that we saw them, fifteen or twenty Vietcong with rifles bunched up in a crowd.

Someone shouted, "There they are!"

I don't know who started firing first. There were muzzle flashes in the night from where the enemy stood, and the crack of bullets over our heads. I told everyone to hold their ground. I shouted for them to stay and fight. I fired my rifle toward the flashes from the enemy's guns and figures in the dark. I went down and fired from one knee. I was very frightened, but I tried to hold my ground. I took a deep breath, forcing myself to stand still and control the fear and panic that had just swept over me.

After the first cracking of the bullets and flashing of their guns, I was now slowly gaining control. My first reaction had been to retreat, but now I began urging the men forward, screaming as loud as I could through the roar of our weapons, all blasting into the night at once. My heart had begun racing through my chest the moment they started shooting at us. We were facing each other off in the dark, a dozen men on each side, rifles and bullets, fifty meters apart. We fired into the crowd of shadows that for a second held their ground too. We had stumbled into each other, the enemy and ourselves in the middle of that moonlit night.

But the men broke and they started running. I yelled for them to stop, but they ran in a panic. I kept firing from my hip, yet they were behind me now, and I raced back trying to catch up with them, still shouting for them to stop: "Keep fighting! Keep fighting, men!" But they kept running backward and soon my courage left me and I began to run with them, the fear now consuming me, back into a ditch in the sand along the beach that was filled with water up to our knees. We had made it, all of us, I thought. The water was cold and my heart was still pounding. Men were screaming and firing their rifles all around me, cursing and swearing; and then, for an instant, it was silent, only the sound of someone running, a figure in the distance, moving toward me in the moonlight.

I had a second to think. "Here they come!" yelled a voice from down in the ditch. "Here they come!" he shouted even louder now. I raise my rifle. He's coming right toward me. He's almost on top of me. I see his gun, a man in the dark coming right at me with a rifle. It was either him or me. I have a second to decide. I raise my rifle. I aim just above my sight. I fire three times. The rifle recoils against my shoulder again and again and again. The attacker falls almost on top of me. He does not move. Have I killed him?

"It's Wilson!" someone shouts. "He's hit!" That one split-second when I heard them call out your name, I felt a jolt, an incredible jolt through my body. It was unlike anything I had ever felt before in my life, followed by a sickening dread. I had just shot one of my own men. I felt weak, as if I was about to faint. I couldn't breathe. Oh my God, oh my God! Do they know I did it? They must, they have to. I was the only one who'd been firing.

They drag your body back into the ditch. Everything is a blur of panic and fear. My God! I lie in the water of the ditch still holding the rifle I shot you with. I don't want to look. I don't want to run over and help. I just shot you, how can I look? They scream, they shout, working feverishly, trying to save you.

"He's hit in the throat!"

As you die before me, it is a nightmare. I hear them screaming as they try to save you, but I feel nothing. Like some horrible dream that I am trapped in that I can't get out of that is just beginning and will never end, never be over for me until I am dead.

"He's still alive!" I hear someone shout.

I've wounded him, I think. I haven't killed him. Better that he was dead! That way no one will know. He'll want to kill me if he survives and finds out I shot him, his own squad leader.

"He's got it in the throat! He's bleeding bad."

I try to block out their words.

"He's still breathing!"

My heart sinks. Why would I ever want him to die? What was I thinking? "How's he doing now?" I suddenly shout into the panic all around me, trying to act as if I'm still the sergeant, still in control, and take the blame away from me.

"He's dying . . . I don't think he's going to make it!" a voice calls out.

Oh live, Wilson . . . please don't die—live! I almost shout. Please, Wilson, live!

"He's dead!"

It hit me like nothing I'd ever felt before, and like nothing I will ever feel again.

"He's dead, Wilson is dead!"

You're gone, dead. I'm in the water, in the ditch, holding the rifle that just killed you. I close my eyes. I don't want to believe this is happening. I want to sink into the sand and die right with you. The panic and fear begin to surge inside me once again. I feel guilt, terror, shame, and anger, all these emotions at once sweeping over me. I look around—no one has accused me. No one has said I did it.

It is a moonlit night in October of 1967 in the DMZ and I have just made the biggest mistake of my life, and no one, not one of my men, has blamed me for your death. But I know soon they will accuse me if I don't do something.

I feel alone and heavy in the ditch. There is silence, an eerie silence along the line of men, and they all seem to be staring at me. What should I do? Should I say I did it? But no one has accused me. Not one of my men has blamed me for your *death. Do they know? Of course they do. They must. But why aren't they saying anything? Why is there this silence?*

I start giving orders, barking commands fiercely to hide my shame and guilty feelings and the awful fear and dread that go with them. What's wrong with them? Don't they know? Don't they realize? Are they too afraid to say what happened? They know! They know! But why, why didn't they say anything that night?

We head back to the battalion area in the amtrac, your lifeless body at my feet, my heart still pounding in my chest. I cannot look down at you. I cannot look. I return to my hooch with the others where I sit on my rack unable to sleep, tormented by guilt and shame.

Shaking with your death still on my hands, and the other men now asleep in their racks around me, I pick up my rifle, raising the barrel to my head. I press the barrel between my eyes and take off my boot, placing my toe on the trigger. Just one push of the trigger with my toe will be all it will take and I will be free from all of this, free from my murdering hands and this awful nightmare that threatens to overwhelm me. One pull of the trigger and I'm free, free from their accusing stares, their looks of disgust.

You fool! *I thought to myself.* How could you have done something so stupid? What about your training? Didn't you learn anything in Marine Corps boot camp? What are you going to tell his parents? What are you going to tell his wife? Oh God . . . Oh Jesus . . .

I sat there in my hooch, the rain still pouring down, the night so dark and low, the coldest moment of my life; everything wrecked, all in a shambles, every dream, every thought and hope, everything learned, every happy moment suddenly crushed in an instant, one night, one mistake, one moment in hell frozen forever; nothing to hold on to. I sat in my hooch that night shivering from your murder, the barrel of my M14 pressed up against my forehead, my toe on the trigger, the other men sleeping in their racks all around me.

As the rain continued to pour onto the corrugated roof of our hooch that night, I struggled to write a letter to your wife.

> Dear Mrs. Wilson,
>   I was the sergeant in charge of your husband's patrol on the night of October 15, 1967. After a firefight with the enemy, he fought bravely, giving us cover as we moved into another position . . .

I tried to explain what happened, why her husband was dead. In the first letter I told your wife everything that happened that night, how we went on patrol and got hit, how we all ran to the ditch, and how you stayed behind fighting the VC. "He was a hero protecting his fellow marines as we moved to another position." I did not tell her that we panicked. I did not say we retreated. Then I lied. I told her you were hit on your way back to our position, shot by the enemy. I told her I was putting you in for a Bronze Star. But I could not finish the letter and I tore it up.

I then began to write a second letter. In this one I decided to tell your wife the truth:

> I don't know how to tell you this, Mrs. Wilson,

but I was the one who killed your husband. I ask you to please forgive me for the awful mistake I have made and what must be the terrible anguish you and your family are feeling at this moment. I am sorry. I am so sorry and I am putting your husband in for a Bronze Star medal.

I started to cry as I wrote that second letter, as I had been unable to cry when I wrote the first.

I just want to tell you I'm sorry, Mrs. Wilson, for what I've done, and I hope you and your family will forgive me. I am so ashamed and I pray and ask God for help and forgiveness.

I finished the letter feeling exhausted and relieved that I had done it. I would send it to her. It is what God would want me to do. I couldn't lie to her. I couldn't keep what happened out there from her. I'll send it, I said to myself, folding it up. I'll send it and be done with all this pain and agony.

But I couldn't send it! I couldn't tell her what had happened. It would be so easy to tell her that you'd been killed by the VC. It was so far away, Georgia, over ten thousand miles. What did they know about Vietnam? What did they know about patrols and firefights? What difference did it make what I told her? Why should I make her feel any worse? You were dead already, weren't you? Why make it any more tragic than it already was?

I was tormented. I had to make a decision.

Then I decided: I sent nothing.

I tore up both of the letters, making certain they were shredded into little bits, not wanting any evidence of what I had done, afraid someone might find my confession and accuse me, knowing for sure that I had killed you.

On only a few rare occasions did I ever come close to revealing to others what happened that night. I did share with my mother the story of how I was wounded, but never did I tell her of the night I shot and killed you. I did all I could to avoid that. The nightmares had already begun, the anxiety attacks, insomnia, and difficulty closing my eyes before I went to sleep at night for fear that I might never wake up.

At the debriefing, I told the major that I had been the one who killed you. I made a full confession, but he would not believe me—though I'm certain he knew—just like the night a few weeks later when we mistakenly shot and wounded the children and killed the old man; and we picked up the pieces of their bodies and put them on the choppers.

A few days later I met a Vietnamese boy named America while on patrol not far from where we killed the old man and wounded the children that night. I wonder what became of that boy. I told him we came to save his country from Communism and that I was sorry for the mistake we had made. We did not know that those we had been sent to protect and save would be the ones we would kill and maim. I spent the entire day with him. He liked me and I wonder if he ever thinks of me after all these years. And the boy whose foot we shot off by mistake? I wonder where he is tonight; I wonder how his mother is.

When the major told me the following morning that the

people we had killed and wounded the night before were VC, I did not believe him. They were innocent civilians, I told him, women and children and an old man we thought were the enemy. I told him I was sick of going out on patrol and that it was hard to tell who the enemy was anymore. Like I said, body count was all that mattered.

The Tent of the Dead

This is the tent of the dead. There is a sign that says, Keep out. Dead American boys are inside. If you look closely, you will see war in its most awful consequence. It is where you were sent after the night I killed you, where you and the others were prepared for your return home. Please, do not go in that tent because you will see the warriors, and you will not like what you see. For you will see them before they have been readied to look good and smell clean, before their bullet and shrapnel holes are patched up and their bloody garments replaced, before their angry stares have been removed, their eyelids pressed down to hide their last scream for life, to cover up their rage at having to leave this world so soon. This is the tent of the dead, where the blood is mopped up and the intestines are put back into place for the long journey home. This is where you were sent, where your body was fixed up and prepared, you, who I killed in that instant of indecision, in that moment of panic and doubt. I pulled the trigger and took a life from this world, so sure you were the enemy. Now you lie in that tent.

MEMORIAL SERVICE

I felt a Funeral, in my Brain,
And Mourners to and fro
Kept treading–treading–till it seemed
That Sense was breaking through–

And when they all were seated,
A Service, like a Drum–
Kept beating–beating–till I thought
My mind was going numb–

—from "I felt a Funeral, in my Brain"
by Emily Dickinson

They held a memorial service for you in a tent not far from the command bunker. I did not want to go but I was afraid that if I didn't show up the others would begin to wonder why. Someone, I think it was Chaplain Edwards, said that you had a wife and a kid and that you were from Georgia. Others spoke of their friendship with you. I tried to block out their words. My heart was pounding in my chest as I sat alone in the back of the tent feeling as if I was about to faint.

* * *

Not long after your death I went to the supply tent where Corporal Ramos was packing up your belongings to send home to your folks. Ramos had been a friend of yours, and as I walked into the tent he stared at me for what seemed a long time. "Can I help you, Sergeant?" he finally said, sounding almost sarcastic.

He knows, I thought to myself, someone told him. "It's too bad about Wilson," I said, trying to sound concerned, but Corporal Ramos did not respond as he continued sorting through your things. I looked down at a photograph of your wife, another that showed you with your mother and father; I saw your sea bag, your shaving kit, a wristwatch, the jungle boots that had been taken off your feet the night you died. I then noticed a small book and asked Corporal Ramos if I could see it.

"You don't want to see that," he said curtly.

It was a slim volume, almost ridiculously slim. How to Stay Alive in Vietnam was the title. How absurd, I thought. How to keep living even though your country has put you in an insane place with rockets and artillery shells raining down on you; How to Stay Alive in Vietnam, how to keep living in this place, this hell, how to stay alive to see your wife, to see your mom and dad, to see your baby who has not yet been born.

How to Stay Alive in Vietnam so that you can take the Freedom Bird home, that plane you dreamed about and imagined and agonized over, that flight out of this place, back to the world again. I opened up the first few pages knowing that this person who I just killed had wanted to survive Vietnam just as much as I did.

I wonder if whoever wrote that book ever went to Vietnam. I wonder if the book has a chapter about being killed by your own sergeant. Maybe they could have called it "The Fuckup Chapter" when something completely crazy and out of the ordinary happens and one of your own men kills you by mistake.

Some of the men in my tent began talking about how the bullet hit you. They said it entered the front of your throat, cutting your jugular vein, and blasted out the back of your head. After they went outside, I stared at my hand for a long time. This is the hand that held the gun, the finger that pulled the trigger and took a life out of this world. With this one finger I ended a life forever.

In a mirror I now see your face in my reflection. It is cold and I am shivering and I dream of redemption, of forgiveness and love. I know I must keep on living. I know I must try. I try to believe again, even in the darkness of this angry room.

A LETTER TO MY MOTHER AND FATHER

November 16, 1967

Dear Folks,

I have something I would like to tell you. I'm going to be a priest. I had my call from God during a firefight last month, and I am certain this is what both my God and I want. God does indeed work in strange ways. The past two months have vastly changed my life and brought me to see things that I never before have seen. I know that it won't be easy, but I know that God wants me to serve him, and he will assist me.

I was a poor student in school and I know this will be working against me, but do you know my faith is so strong that I don't worry? I know the Lord my God will guide me and sustain me. I ask for your prayers in order to help me pursue my vocation. Remember, I pray for you always. I am now in charge of fourteen scouts and am platoon sergeant. I have a great bunch of men, and I am proud of every one of them. The responsibility I now have is as if a ton of

bricks have been dropped on top of me; fourteen lives
in my hands.

In God is my trust,
Ron

WOUNDING

January 20, 1968

We are sweeping toward the village across a wide and open area of sand. We will be the point of the attack for the captain and the battalion behind us. Others already forming will sweep south from the graveyard north of the village. This time I promise myself there will be no retreat.

I feel the small Bible in the top pocket of my utility jacket and touch the rosary beads around my neck. I kiss the crucifix, saying a short prayer that I might make it through the attack alive. We are halfway across the open area when rounds start cracking all around my head. We are getting hit. I fire full automatic bursts back into the village. Some of the others run for the tree line near the river, diving for cover. I keep moving forward, changing magazines, dropping empty ones into the sand. There is nothing to shoot at but I keep firing anyway, rounds still crackling around me and ripping into the sand at my feet.

There is a sudden shock, and for a moment in the war, time has stopped. I am hit. My leg is numb. I can't feel anything from my knee down. I look at my foot. There is a gaping hole in the back of my heel. I think of running back, but I stay there out in the open with the bullets still flying everywhere. I fall into a prone position. I am trying to fire my rifle but it is jamming, filled with sand. I try to put a new round into the chamber. Maybe I can fire one at a time. But it is all useless. I am caught in the open with a rifle that no longer works. There is nothing left but to get out of there. I start to get up. Something explodes next to my right ear. A bullet tears through my right shoulder and lung, smashing into my spine.

January 22, 1968

The dead and dying are everywhere. I am in and out of morphine every four hours, awakening to the screams of the wounded all around me. I am told by a doctor that I will never walk again, that I will be in a wheelchair for the rest of my life. Still, I am grateful to be alive, to be breathing. I dream of my hometown, of my mother, father, and the backyard where I once played as a boy. In many ways I think this wound is my punishment for killing you that night. I have been sentenced to life imprisonment in a body that will be dead from my mid-chest down for as long as I live. Finally, the score has been evened up.

I completely lose track of time. I don't know if it is day or night. They keep bringing in the wounded and carting out the dead. It is January 1968, the eve of the Tet Offensive. A young Vietnamese man who has been severely wounded is brought into the intensive care ward and placed in a bed directly across from me. I look at his face and see the fear in his eyes. One of the nurses tells me he is a Vietcong soldier who was shot in the chest only a few days ago.

He's the enemy, I think to myself, *the Vietcong, the "gook," the Communist my country sent me to fight and kill; the one I must fear, the one I must hate, a man who is not even human.* This belief and hatred were reinforced in boot camp at Parris Island, South Carolina, where we had chanted, "I'm going to go to Vietnam, I'm going to kill the yellow man!"

Perhaps he is the one who pulled the trigger a few days ago, trying to kill me, the one who shot and paralyzed me from my mid-chest down for the rest of my life. I will never know for sure. Yet, as I lie in my hospital bed and our eyes meet, I feel no hatred or animosity toward him. On the contrary I feel . . . compassion.

Each day upon awakening from the morphine, we look at each other, never a word being spoken, just our eyes meeting, a gaze, a recognition of each other's presence, our humanity, an understanding that both of our worlds have been turned upside down and we are now in a far different place than we were only a few days ago. We have reached an equality of sorts in this place of the wounded and dying; that great leveler, where distinctions vanish, where there is no prejudice or hatred, where everything becomes equal. We are two severely wounded young men in late January 1968 simply trying to survive, two human beings who only want to live.

A sort of unique bond begins to develop between my "enemy" and myself over the next several days, a strange and at first somewhat uneasy camaraderie without words, which is unsettling but also feels completely natural to me.

I begin to think of him more and more as a friend, and each time I awake from the morphine with the screams of the wounded and dying all around me, I reach out to him as he lies across from me in his bed. *Keep fighting*, I think as I look into his eyes, trying to communicate with my facial expression. I want him to know that I care, that there is no longer any hatred or animosity between us, that I want him to live just as much as I want to live.

We are together in this now, and none of those other things matter anymore; we are two young men simply trying to survive, to return home and leave the war behind forever. *Don't give up!* I tell him with my eyes. *I won't give up if you don't give up! I'll keep fighting if you keep fighting!*

The lights are always on and I never know if it is night or day, and after a while it doesn't really matter anymore. I awake one day and look across and see an empty hospital bed. He is gone and the nurse tells me he has died. There is no emotion in her voice. She is very tired and there will be many more dead and wounded before this is all over.

I stare at his empty bed for a long time, feeling a sadness that I cannot fully comprehend.

In the years that have passed, I have often thought about those days on the intensive care ward, and about that young Vietnamese man, and how we are all perhaps much closer to each other as brothers and sisters on this earth than we realize. Despite all our differences, there is, I believe, a powerful connectedness to our humanity—a deep desire to reach out with kindness, with love and great caring toward each other, even to our supposed enemies, and to bring forth "the better angels of our nature." That is undeniable and cannot be extinguished, even in death.

There is the long flight home packed with wounded men all around me, every conceivable and horrifying wound you can imagine. Even the unconscious and those whose brains have been blown apart by bullets and shrapnel make the ride with me because we are all going home now, and this is only the beginning. The frustration, rage, insomnia, nightmares, anxiety attacks, terrible restlessness, and desperate need to keep moving will come later, but for now we are so thankful to have just made it out of that place, so grateful to be alive even with these grievous wounds.

ALONE IN OUR ROOMS

Spring 1969

We are alone in our rooms. This is the part you never see, the part that is never reported in the news, the part that the president and vice president never mention. This is the agonizing part, the lonely part, the hurting part when you have to wake to the wound each morning and suddenly realize what you've lost, what is gone forever.

They have mothers and fathers, sisters and brothers, husbands and wives, and they're not saying much right now. Like me, they're just trying to get through each day, trying to be brave and not cry. We are still extremely grateful to be alive, but slowly we are beginning to realize what has happened to us.

BREAKING THE CRUCIFIX

After the war there was no God and for him there was no country anymore.

I t is the late spring of 1969 and I sit in my room staring down at the plastic crucifix I hold in my hand. It all seems to be making sense this morning, all the pieces are beginning to fit together. God is dead! There is no heaven. There is no hell. It's all made up. It's nothing but a fucking lie!

I am having conflicting feelings. A part of me is ready, while another part isn't sure. I would be breaking with my past, all my beliefs, my God, my country, my mother and father, the church—all that they taught me, all that I have ever believed in. For several months now, ever since I began taking classes at the university, I have felt myself slowly beginning to awaken, as if from a terrible nightmare, a nightmare so vast and complicated that only now can I begin to fathom the depth of my betrayal. Perhaps it is the fact that I have sustained such a horrific and devastating wound that I am thinking these thoughts. *Who is this Christ anyway, this Savior, this*

*King of Kings who supposedly died for our sins? Jesus was
nailed to the cross for three days, but I will have to hang from
my cross for the rest of my life.*

I look down again at the crucifix. What for so long
and for so many years seemed to soothe me and give
me comfort now torments me. My mind drifts back to
a beautiful spring day when I was a boy in Levittown,
Long Island. I was walking along the sidewalk repeating, "I love you, Jesus, I love you, Jesus," bowing my
head each time I said his name. I kept repeating this
in almost a whisper as I headed toward the A&P supermarket on Hempstead Turnpike where my father
worked as a checker.

I can hear the sound of my mother turning on the
vacuum cleaner in the living room. I always loved that
sound, that soft hum that as a boy made me feel safe and
secure, just like the crucifix I now hold in my hands. I
think back to the veterans hospital in the Bronx when
I would paint pictures of the crucifix with myself as
Christ, and how they sent the psychiatrist down from
the psych ward because they were concerned, and I immediately stopped painting, afraid they would have me
committed like my Uncle Paul who was beaten to death
in a mental hospital years before.

When I first came home from the hospital, my mother
and father did all they could to make me comfortable.
My father built a beautiful wooden ramp in the front
of our house. My mother contacted our parish priest,
Father Cassidy, to ensure that I would receive Holy Communion as I was wheeled through the front door.

My parents also moved a special bed given to them by the VA into my room. This bed, which is just like the one in the hospital, has an overhead trapeze that enables me to keep my balance and transfer my paralyzed body in and out of it. It is all electric and plugged into the wall. The bed can be lowered or raised and tilted in different angles by the push of a button. On the wall, just above the headboard, my mother has placed a plastic crucifix. The crucifix is the first thing I see every morning upon awakening and I often begin each day by praying to Jesus. Yet as time goes by, the more I look at Jesus hanging from the cross, the more hideous it all seems. I continue staring down at the crucifix, I wonder why it has taken me so long to realize these things. Why haven't I been able to see this Christ, this crucifix, for what it really is? Did it take my savage wounding in the war to finally open my eyes, or was it that night when I pulled the trigger of my M14 and killed you?

I was used like all the others throughout the centuries, like all the dead whose names are on walls and monuments. The silent dead, the ones who will never speak, the nineteen- and twenty-year-olds like me who the government has sent to fight their wars and gotten killed. What would the dead say if they could speak, if for just one moment they could scream from those statues and monuments? There is no God, no Jesus. It is all a fucking lie; the priests, the nuns, all the authority figures. It is all a fraud, a fucking weird dream attached to a radiator that just keeps getting hotter and hotter; a fairy tale told by a bunch of madmen.

The time to act has finally come. I take a long, deep breath, convinced now more than ever of what I am about to do. Just when I'm about to scream, I snap the crucifix in two. There, I did it! *I'm finally free!* I feel like I have just freed myself from a terrible lie, like a prisoner who has escaped from a cell he has been in his whole life.

I sit there holding the broken crucifix in my hands, thinking about what I've just done. Only moments ago, I was thrilled to have finally broken with my past, but now I am feeling guilty, like that awful night in the war.

It is as if I've just committed a murder and need to find a way to hide the body. Where will I put these two pieces of the crucifix, where will I hide this broken body of Christ? I try flushing them down the toilet, but they keep getting stuck, and after several attempts I finally reach down into the bowl with my bare hand and pull the two pieces out. I dry them off with a towel, then return to my room and pull out my high school jock strap from my chest of drawers. After carefully wrapping the broken pieces of Jesus in my jock strap and placing them in my chest of drawers, I leave the room.

THE BLACK SPOT

March 1982

Sometimes the material I was working on would make me depressed. I'd have anxiety attacks and feel as if I was about to die. My heart would start palpitating and I'd have chest pains that made me wonder if I was having a heart attack. I'd become frightened and would push out of my hotel room in a panic, leaving the door wide open and rushing down to the ocean, all the way out to the end of the pier where the Mexican guys and their kids would be fishing.

The fish they caught would be flopping around on the wet concrete pier and I'd scream at the top of my lungs. The Mexican guys would look at me like I was crazy. I'd wave my hand at them as if to say, *Don't worry, I'm okay, just letting out a little steam.* I'd take deep breaths and stare out into the vast Pacific, wondering if I was ever going to survive the writing of this book and keep from going crazy.

I sit before your grave, looking down at the small white stone that is your marker. The rain drips slowly off your headstone.

Tiny droplets form on the shriveled bud of a rose put there by someone who loved you: your wife, your mother, your father? They must still come back after all these years to be with you, to remember you.

Time: all the years, what difference does it make, all the time that passes? How can you ever forget someone you bore from your womb, someone you raised and loved all those years, your child? All that time makes no difference. You will always be.

Let the dead rest. I can't bring you back. I can't change that night. I must let you go. Let it all go. Get on with my life. Stop living in the past.

Perhaps it was the black spot on my face in the high school yearbook. Even back then I saw it as some kind of sign or omen that I was marked for something tragic and awful, and the terrible things that had happened in the war seemed to confirm this. I was separate from all the rest. That spot, that terrible mark was there, permanent, forever, and there was nothing I could do about it. The guy at the yearbook store said they were sorry. They had no idea how that ink spot had gotten on my graduation photo. I felt ashamed and deeply scarred. None of the other students' graduation photos had a spot. Why did this have to happen to me? Why couldn't I be like everybody else?

Clearly the odds were stacked against me. I had been a poor student in high school. I had failed most of my subjects in my senior year and was forced to go to summer school, not to mention that I wasn't allowed to graduate with the rest of my class.

I can still remember how humiliated I felt as I peered through that rusty chain-link fence at the school's baseball field with tears in my eyes, watching the class of '64 graduate in their caps and gowns without me. I'd been left behind and would have to go to summer school, where in the sweltering heat of that terrible Long Island summer I would sit behind my desk making up for my failure.

And yet, despite all of my terrible doubts, everything that a fortune-teller in Venice said one afternoon seemed to renew my confidence. Sitting behind her card table on Ocean Front Walk, she looked into my eyes and told me that I would someday write "the Great American Novel." She said, "There is no doubt about it. You will be showered with acclaim. Your fame will be far and wide, and millions will know your name!" She explained this with such fierce conviction that I believed her immediately. Her words touched me deeply, and in a world without God, she gave me hope.

Yes, I thought to myself, *this will all come to pass, this is all meant to be.*

It was without question in the stars. My mother had seen it in a dream and I had sensed it in a premonition once while I was at church; and now I had the fortune-teller's reading in Venice.

I wanted to believe her. I *needed* to believe her, needed to believe that things could be better, that miracles were still possible, that tragedies such as mine could be overcome.

Maybe the black spot on my face in the high school

yearbook was not the mark of humiliation and defeat; on the contrary, perhaps it revealed my destiny, the sign of a man marked for something great.

PART III

THE LONG JOURNEY HOME

Burned out and exhausted and having spent several months trying to write the Great American Novel, I left LA in the late spring of 1982 and headed up to San Francisco. Immediately upon arriving, I checked into the York Hotel on Sutter Street. It was my favorite place to stay whenever I went to the Bay Area; an almost exclusively gay-run hotel with beautiful turn-of-the-century marble floors, winding *Gone with the Wind*–style staircase, a cherrywood banister, and the infamous Plush Room which boasted nightly entertainment, everything from bawdy drag queens to the talented actress and singer Eartha Kitt.

I believe I was the only straight guy staying there at the time, but I always felt welcome. The AIDS epidemic had not yet fully reared its angry head and San Francisco still pulsated with a tremendous energy that was nothing short of breathtaking. Each night I would catch a cab over to North Beach where I would go to Enrico's Café on Broadway for dinner, then push my wheelchair down the street to Lawrence Ferlinghetti's City Lights Bookstore and hang out for hours, fascinated with its history and eclectic selection of books, including Jack Kerouac's *On the Road* and Allen Ginsberg's *Howl*, not to mention the authors, artists, and poets who would drop by from time to time.

And it was at City Lights one night that I ran into Nancy Peters, who, along with Ferlinghetti, was co-owner of the legendary bookstore, as well as a terrific editor who had once worked at the Library of Congress in Washington, DC. I explained to Nancy that I had just returned from Paris and had been living at a hotel in LA and working on a novel but had decided to head up to the Bay Area for some much-needed rest. I then told her that I wanted to do a little painting and wondered if she knew of anyone interested in renting a place to me, preferably a cottage over the Golden Gate Bridge in Marin County where I could hopefully find some peace and quiet.

Nancy seemed to completely understand. "I think I've got just the place you're looking for, Ron," she said, explaining that just that morning she had received a call from a friend of Ferlinghetti's named Suzanne Shelhart who worked for the Paris Realty Company. She'd told Nancy that a beautiful little cottage in Sausalito had just come up for rent and to please call back if she knew of anyone who might be interested.

It was charming place, a block from Richardson Bay on Turney Street, directly in back of a house owned by an elderly woman named Karen Marlow, and I fell in love with it immediately. I wasn't quite ready to get back to

writing the Great American Novel, and painting might
be a way to continue expressing myself without feeling
so isolated and depressed.

I dream my painting and I paint my dream.
–Vincent van Gogh

Whatever artistic gifts I may have, I believe came
from my mother's side of our family. Her mother Mary,
in addition to raising five children during the Great Depression, was a prolific artist and one of her many oil
paintings hung in the hallway of our house in Massapequa for many years. Both of Mom's brothers, Dick
and Jim, who served in the marines during World War
II and Korea, were gifted artists too—Uncle Jimmy was
a cartoonist and Dick a writer who would go on to publish several books on religion and faith. My mother's
sister Betty, a Catholic nun, was also talented and made
a beautiful pen-and-ink portrait of me as a young boy
that I still have today.

My mother loved to write too, and though she wrote
nearly a dozen books in her lifetime and had dreams
of publishing a great book someday, none were ever
accepted by a publisher. I recall discovering numerous rejection letters over the years in my mother's top
drawer, politely and tactfully written by editors or their
trusted assistants, explaining why the book hadn't been
accepted and almost always encouraging my mother to
not give up and keep trying, which is exactly what she
did right up to the last year of her life, hoping, always

hoping and praying, that her next book would be the one that a big New York publishing house would finally accept. Though I do remember one rejection letter which both angered me and brought tears to my eyes, stating that the unscrupulous editor's assistant would read my mother's manuscript only if she would be willing to pay a fee in order to "defer the cost of my valuable time." My father did eventually pay to publish one book of my mother's entitled *Moma*, about my father's Yugoslavian immigrant mother Anna Kovacevich and her life on a rural dairy farm in northern Wisconsin during the Great Depression, which sold few if any books but did make excellent Christmas gifts for family members and friends.

When I was still quite young, my father gathered us all in the living room of our house in Massapequa and said that my mother had decided to take "a little trip" and would not be back for several weeks, if not months. Little did we know at the time that she had suffered a serious mental breakdown and her little trip was to a local psychiatric hospital where she was given a series of electroshock treatments for her growing depression. She did eventually recover but battled with alcoholism and periods of depression for most of her adult life, going on and off the wagon—yet despite these personal and emotional demons, through it all she continued to write, had an unflagging spirit, razor-sharp wit, and a wicked "Irish" sense of humor. At the time of her death, she had compiled nearly five thousand pages of books, plays, and poems, all written in her inimitable style, often defying convention and in a language all her own.

My grandmother Mary's first husband, James Lamb, despite having been shell-shocked and gassed during World War I, became a successful high school principal in one of Brooklyn's toughest neighborhoods, not to mention a poet and artist who tragically died of alcoholism at the age of thirty-nine.

My grandmother once told me that Jim had been born on the third of July and was deeply disappointed that he had missed the fourth by one day. "He was so patriotic and would have been very happy to know that one of his grandsons was born on the Fourth of July," she told me one day in her backyard. I never got the chance to meet my grandfather but often wondered what it might have been like to spend time with him. Not long after I left the VA hospital in the Bronx, I found an old composition notebook in my mother's top bedroom drawer filled with poems he had written in the years following World War I. The writing was very patriotic and filled with great passion for a country he truly loved even though he had been deeply traumatized by his war experiences. One of his poems was about World War I veterans marching down Broadway in New York City on Memorial Day in 1921. Despite his large body of work, I could sense between the lines a deeply troubled man who was struggling to find his way home from the horrors of that war.

My Uncle Paul, who suffered from schizophrenia, and who my grandmother Mary was convinced was a genius, would often entertain us with his wild and imaginative stories told right off the top of his head whenever we visited my grandmother's house. He was tragically murdered in a Long Island mental asylum, beaten to death by one of his fellow inmates. A closed coffin at the wake was necessary due to Uncle Paul's massive head wounds. Ancient Gregorian chants (Paul's favorites) could be heard softly playing over and over again on a record player provided by the funeral home's director. Most of my family, a Catholic priest, and several nuns who my aunt Betty invited from her convent attended, with me standing alone at attention next to the coffin in my dress blue uniform, just back from my first tour of duty in Vietnam.

I thought back to my own experiences at the Bronx VA hospital after breaking my right femur while exercising at my apartment in Hempstead, Long Island, and how out of sheer frustration, while trapped in a body cast for nearly six months, I began painting myself as Christ hanging from the cross. When this led the hospital staff to bring in a psychiatrist, I simply stopped painting.

But now, thousands of miles from that depressing hospital ward in the Bronx, I would no longer be afraid; at Karen Marlow's cottage, I would be free to paint and write whatever came to my mind, and no one would stop me.

The Art Store
The art store was a few blocks from the cottage, and with

the few hundred dollars I had left from my monthly disability check, I wheeled over one afternoon to buy as many supplies as I could carry. When I entered the store, I was met by an attractive young woman named Ann. "Can I help you?" she asked with a smile. I told her that I was planning to do a lot of painting, and she seemed to immediately sense my desperation.

As she led me down a long aisle filled with art supplies, I picked up an empty canvas, imagining all the paintings I would do that spring. I felt like telling her, *I need to start right now! I won't be any bother. I'll pay for all the paint and supplies, just let me begin right here in your store. I can't wait another minute!* As far as I was concerned, there was no end to all the paintings I had inside of me.

I filled two large plastic bags with supplies and carried them back to the cottage. It was a miracle that I was able to get down the block in my wheelchair with those two bags on my lap, nearly blinding me. I somehow managed to push myself up the steep ramp in front of Karen's house, past the beautiful oak tree with a rope swing, and along the winding path beside tall bamboo shoots that always reminded me of Vietnam.

As soon as I entered the cottage, I tore open the two plastic bags, intending to paint the first thing that came to mind. I looked out the open door at the bright afternoon sunshine. On a large bush in front of the cottage, I spotted a beautiful red rose that had bloomed earlier that morning. I studied it for several minutes and then with a squish from a tube of red acrylic paint, I created my very first painting, *Impression of a Rose*.

By that evening I had painted nearly a dozen red roses, all done very quickly and with great passion, as if I were shouting to the world that I was alive, still here, and that I hadn't been defeated. I then grabbed for more tubes of paint and soon completed a brightly colored abstract painting of flowers in bloom with a giant bee buzzing above them. I felt exhilarated, and by the next morning I had completed almost thirty different paintings of various sizes and shapes.

Rules and regulations concerning art and painting seemed ridiculous to me. I just wanted to throw paint onto canvas as quickly as I could. *Fuck the easel* was my attitude. *Fuck the paintbrush too!* I was a whole different breed, a whole new rebel artist just back from a war, expressing myself with those tubes of paint as directly and immediately as possible, as if to say, *I might die at any moment.* Death was always just around the corner.

I scribbled in my diary,

I've been to the very edge overlooking the abyss and I've looked out and seen nothing but darkness and despair and I'm painting from that place, that ledge that goes on forever and falls into nothingness, and is eternal and endless and immortal as the sun and the moon and the stars, and my expressions, my paintings, come from that place, that moment in Vietnam when I almost died, and my bright colors from the light that was almost taken away from me; the knowledge that life is short, too short sometimes, and that every second counts, every moment matters.

I worked all night long with little concern for my health. I couldn't get enough papers and canvases, enough tubes of paint. I kept going back and forth between the art store and the cottage, feeling as if a ton of paper, a warehouse of paper, wouldn't be enough for all the paintings I had inside of me.

I wanted to make beautiful and hopeful paintings representing a new beginning. Alone in the cottage each night with my art, I could get away from the memories of Vietnam, and sometimes even the nightmares would leave me for a while.

We express our being by creating. Creativity
is a necessary sequel to being.
—Rollo May

I was willing to try anything, and I thought back
to a book by the psychologist Rollo May, *The Courage
to Create.* I had never read the entire book, but it was
the title that I identified with most. *This is who I am,* I
scrawled on the back of one of my paintings. *This is my
expression, in this place, in this time, with this canvas and
tube of paint. This is my life, my heartbeat that they could not
destroy. This is the way I see the world. This is what life is to
me, these colors, these strokes, these twisted forms and brightly
colored abstract expressions that have come from my hand and
my heart. This is my interpretation of this day, this moment
in my life.*

Hours would go by as if no time had passed at all, just
my expression and color and all that force and energy
put behind every toss of my hand, squeezing the paint
out of the tube and sometimes splattering it across the
canvas. My work was often primal, almost childlike: a
huge tree with violent slashes of brown and green next
to a giant yellow sun recklessly painted with a wild swirl
as if it were about to fly off into the universe.

I was happier than I'd been in a long time. It was a
relief to not be writing about Vietnam, and I thought
that if I never wrote another word, another paragraph
about it, for the rest of my life, that would be all right
with me. Those tubes of paint seemed to represent

something liberating to me, something related to my very survival; each time I threw paint onto canvas, I moved further away from the horrors of that war. *That's what art is about,* I wrote in my diary. *That's what this artistic expression is—a man who could not paint enough bright colors, who could not express enough hope for all the darkness he had seen, for all the agony and sorrow he had been forced to endure.*

I painted each night until dawn, sensing the cold chill of death always close, yet still reaching out to the light, to a new beginning; meeting death on that strange battlefield deep within and slaying it time and time again with each desperate toss of my hand.

> *I put my heart and my soul into my work, and*
> *have lost my mind in the process.*
> —Vincent van Gogh

And now I had finally done it, a torrent of work, over three hundred and fifty paintings: crucifixes, flowers blooming, simple images with the brightest colors I could find. I loved the reds and yellows and blues and deep purples.

I was willing to try anything. One afternoon I threw paint on top of a large sheet of blank watercolor paper I had laid on the cottage floor, then wheeled around and around in my chair, creating a wild collage of circles and colors. I made one painting with toothpaste, after having run out of paints, and I can still remember how it smelled, and how it made me laugh when I awoke several days later to find it covered with ants devouring the tasty fluoride.

I then made several collages. I took an old *Sgt. Rock* comic book and pasted different images onto a large sheet of paper, resulting in a powerful statement against the war. I did a whole Boy Scout series, having gotten ahold of an old handbook at a garage sale. I ripped the pages out and pasted them onto a plywood backing, producing a sarcastic statement about how easily young people are seduced by the romance of war.

There was another series where I created dozens of American flags in all the colors of the rainbow to symbolize a more peaceful and hopeful country. On one flag I wrote, *A NEW NATION IS BEING BORN FROM ALL THOSE PIECES TATTERED AND TORN!* Another flag, less hopeful, expressed my anger and frustration—in bold black letters scrawled across its red, white, and blue surface, it shouted, *DIVORCE*, followed by, *SORROW, TROUBLE*, and, *HOW MUCH MORE CAN I ENDURE?*

At some point I began writing short stories, poems, and plays as well, sometimes while lying on my bed in the cottage with a pillow under my chest. One short story, "The Recruiters," which was eventually published years later, was about two Marine Corps recruiters who come to speak at a high school class only to admit to the young boys in the audience that they had been castrated by "a little Vietnamese guy" after betting their balls in a game of pool.

I also began several novellas in the days that followed: *A Baseball Story*, *Jobo's Clock*, and *The Death of the American Family*. *American Trash* was a paste-up book consisting of unpaid traffic tickets, rejection letters from publishers, threatening notices from bill collectors, and a piece of crumpled toilet paper. I showed *American Trash* to my friend Richie and he laughed at me, telling me I was crazy and that I had really gone over the edge this time, but this didn't bother me. Later that same afternoon, Richie allowed me to do a portrait of him using a charcoal pencil. I still have that portrait today, and each time I look at it I think of Richie and smile.

It was one of the most prolific periods of my life—the paintings, short stories, novellas, poems, and plays were now piled everywhere in the cottage, with splatters of paint on the floor that I had been unable to scrape up. I was afraid that Karen might walk in and see her beautiful cottage turned into some kind of wild artist's studio.

I was making love to every canvas, to each page, sometimes almost savagely, frantically, violently.

THE WAR IS OVER:
A CELEBRATION OF LIFE

December 1982

After a bit of coaxing from my friend Janet Bernie, I decided to finally show my work. The flyer read, *The War Is Over: A Celebration of Life, paintings by Ron Kovic.* No matter how much I had lost, no matter how much physical and emotional pain I had been forced to endure, I was finally leaving the war behind and nearly every one of my paintings symbolized that desire to begin anew, to move beyond all the sorrow and believe again in a world that for so long had felt distant and cold.

Many of my paintings were like precious children I would never have because of my paralysis, children I had been involved with intimately for many nights and days that spring. A part of me didn't want to move them to the café, a strange foreign place where they could not be protected. At least in the cottage I knew they were safe. I would come home to them every night and they would give me great comfort, many of them still drying from the night before, thumbtacked to the walls. I was afraid of what might happen at the exhibit and how someone might try to steal one of them, yet at the same time I was proud to have been offered the opportunity to show my work and, by doing so, perhaps reach others like myself who were still struggling to come home from that war.

It took several trips across the Golden Gate Bridge in Janet's station wagon to move all the paintings to a room I got at the Holiday Inn on Van Ness Avenue, not far from the Chelsea Café on Polk Street, where my art opening was to be held the following week.

With the help of Janet and some other friends, I covered the walls of the café with my art. I don't think the owner had any idea I was going to put up so many paintings, but when I finished there must have been close to a hundred of them. I didn't have the money—or the time, for that matter—to frame each painting, though it would have been nice. I did feel a little uncomfortable at first putting them up with Scotch tape hinges the way you'd put a stamp into a collector's album, but what the hell, it was my art, my expression. I felt better about this when someone in the café told me that the hanging technique seemed to give each one of my paintings a "raw and primal" immediacy.

A woman who came to the opening night of the exhibition seemed quite disturbed by my art; she said she felt dizzy and was convinced the paintings had been done by a madman in an insane asylum. I tried not to let her comments bother me. Another elderly gentleman complained that the paintings were upsetting his peace of mind and giving him heart palpitations, and demanded they be taken down immediately. But for the most part, people seemed impressed.

After it was all over that night, I went back to my room at the Holiday Inn feeling wonderful inside. The show had been a success and I could not remember feeling happier or more alive in a long time. My paintings stayed up on the walls of the Chelsea Café for another three weeks, the owner telling me it was good for business.

In the weeks that followed, I tried to get back to painting, but for some reason I became frustrated. Where for months that extremely prolific period had seemed to sustain me, I now grew depressed, and my beautiful cottage began to feel like a prison.

I couldn't sleep at night and began to worry that I might be dying. I can't explain it but something deep inside me was crying out for love, for someone to hold me close at night. I went to the Chart House restaurant every night for dinner and watched the young waitresses in their short skirts, imagining one of them agreeing to go home with me, but that never happened.

One evening I tried writing a poem:

> I am alone in the cottage and I have grown so sick and
> tired of being alone,
> so horny and sex starved that I fear I may go mad.
> I need human comfort.

What must I do to be touched, rob a bank?
Shoot someone?
Will handcuffs touch me?
Will prison bars feel?

Almost every night before going to bed I'd turn on the Playboy Channel and masturbate before the flickering screen, wetting my index finger and rubbing my left nipple back and forth, then scream into my pillow, trying to relieve my growing sexual tension. The nightmares and anxiety attacks which had plagued me for years and seemed to disappear during that period of painting and writing at the cottage now returned with a vengeance.

Clearly, I had been running a race against myself, and I began to sense that I was about to lose that race. All those frightening thoughts and nightmares I had delayed were pounding on my cottage door, seeking me out and threatening my very existence. Every fear, every demon and ghost that had ever haunted me in the years after the war, were now surrounding my cottage—on the roof, underneath the floor—tormenting me and forcing me to face what I had not wanted to face.

I had been obsessed with the fear of an early death, for years convinced I would not live past my thirtieth birthday, certain I would die young and never reach my true destiny, and now it was all closing in. Could I somehow avoid having to face those fears? Was there a way to truly leave Vietnam behind and be happy again?

Ever since that decision at Jacques's apartment in

Paris to write the Great American Novel, I had been trying to confront the nightmare of that war. Now, as I lay awake with insomnia, tossing and turning and screaming into my pillow, I knew it was time to leave the cottage and, in doing so, avoid the frightening monster that was chasing me. The only question was: where would I go next?

TRACERS

Summer 1985

My friend and fellow Vietnam veteran John
DiFusco called from LA to tell me that he
had just been contacted by Tom Bird at the
VETCo (Veterans Ensemble Theatre Company) office
in New York City. Bird said that the producer Joseph
Papp wanted to bring John's Vietnam play *Tracers* to the
Public Theater in Greenwich Village. "We're going to
New York City, brother!" John shouted over the phone.

That was the last time I talked to him before I
heard that *Tracers* had become a big success. I tried to
reach him several times by phone to congratulate him
but wasn't able to get ahold of him; I suspected he was
probably caught up in all the excitement. A few days
later I spoke with Tom Bird, who told me that he was
just heading out of his office to meet with John at the
Public Theater, and that *Tracers* was playing to packed
audiences almost every night. I asked Tom to give my
regards to John and have him call me.

About a week later John called, sounding all out of

breath and telling me how happy he was to hear from me. He insisted that I leave San Francisco immediately and join him and the rest of the *Tracers* cast in New York City. "We need you're support, brother," he said. "The guys would love to see you. It's fucking crazy here. You're not going to believe what's happening, man. We're packing them in every night!"

I told him it would take me a few days to get ready but he could count on me to head back east as soon as I could. John's call and invitation came as a great relief. My depression and the terrible rut I'd fallen into at the cottage seemed to suddenly lift, and I immediately began making plans for the big trip. I was able to quickly arrange with a friend to sublet the cottage, with the understanding that if I decided to return sooner than expected, the place could be waiting for me on short notice.

Maybe New York and John's play would be the tonic I needed. The feeling that I wasn't going to live much longer continued to permeate my whole being. The poems I had written after my art exhibit ended were reflections of a very bitter man who saw less and less hope in life, a man with his back against the wall. Maybe in New York I would finally find love. All I knew was just that I needed to make a change, and soon, before I went crazy.

New York City

When I arrived at JFK International Airport several days later, I caught a cab into Manhattan and checked into the Edison Hotel. I had stayed at the Edison several times over the years, having first discovered it in the early '70s. Officially opened in 1931, and located in the heart of Times Square, the hotel had grown a bit seedy over the years but still had that old-fashioned charm of its heyday.

I was given my favorite room on the seventeenth floor that was quiet and peaceful, though it didn't have much of a view other than a few tall buildings and flashing neon signs. The bellmen were some of the most down-to-earth people I had ever met, true New Yorkers in every respect with their gruff voices and fast-paced manner that startled many tourists, yet seemed completely normal to me. Most had been employed at the Edison for decades.

I was a long way from the cottage in Sausalito but less than an hour's drive to my old neighborhood in Massapequa, Long Island. It was comforting and felt like home.

The Play

I got to the theater around six p.m. and wheeled into the lobby, where I was met by a kind woman who said she would let John know I had arrived. A few minutes later John appeared, very excited to see me. He gave me a big hug and said that the "tribe," which the all–Vietnam veteran cast had been calling themselves since their opening night at the Odyssey Theatre in Santa Monica, was "psyched up" over the fact that I was there that night. "It really means a lot to them that you came, brother!"

The year before in Santa Monica, the cast had dedicated their opening-night performance to me on my birthday. As grateful as I was for this recognition, I hadn't actually attended opening night or any other performance of *Tracers*, afraid that the play might be too much for me to take. But now, here I was in New York City at Joseph Papp's Public Theater, finally ready to see the show.

John had reserved a special place for me right up front, and although I appreciated the respect, I felt trapped and wondered if I'd be able to escape from the performance if I felt overwhelmed. For years I had been running and hiding, deflecting and denying, desperately doing all I could to avoid the ghost that was chasing me. I had hoped I could sit in the back row where no one would notice if I tried to leave, but now I was right up front where everyone could see me, and I didn't want to embarrass John or the others by taking off in the middle of the show.

They had made such a big deal about the fact that I was in the audience that I knew I had to stay. I could close my eyes, but I could not stick my fingers in my ears, something I would do when I didn't want to hear people talking about Vietnam or the war.

As the lights dimmed and the play began, I was surprised by my initial reaction; rather than feeling a need to escape, my fears vanished, and I found myself drawn into the story. Perhaps it was the actors gyrating wildly onstage to a crazy and maddening beat. Or maybe it was one of the later scenes when actor–Vietnam veteran Vincent Caristi, portraying the character Baby San, said, "I lost my judgment the other day. I killed a man and now Brooklyn seems like a world away," sending chills down my spine and reminding me of my own horrifying night in the war.

John invited me backstage after the play and gathered us all into a circle where we held each other tightly for a long time. I had been so afraid of seeing *Tracers*, but now I sensed that something deep within my soul had begun to heal.

MONA

John called the hotel one afternoon to tell me that
he had just been invited to the opening of another
play about Vietnam by a small off-Broadway group
at a place in Greenwich Village called the People's Theater. John asked if I'd be interested in joining him and
said that there would probably be some "good-looking
ladies" in the play.

I was hesitant at first, but then I thought, *Why not?*
Having been in the city now for over a month, I was
starting to feel a bit lonely, especially on the so-called
"dark nights" when there weren't any performances of
Tracers. Most of the time I'd stay in my room at the Edison trying to paint or watching TV, but I was growing
restless and knew I needed to get out. I told John I'd
love to join him, and as soon as I got off the phone I
began to imagine meeting a cute actress at the theater,
perhaps someone I could get involved with.

The following evening, I took the hotel elevator to
the ground floor, rubbing and twisting my left nipple
until I felt like I was going to scream. I had not been
with a woman in a long time and the thought of that

possibility filled me with excitement. Who knew what might come of this night? In any event, I wasn't going to hide in my room any longer—what kind of life was that?

I had made an important decision the previous evening to meet life head-on regardless of the consequences. I understood that there was risk involved, but there comes a time when you get so sick and tired of being alone, a virtual prisoner of your fears, trapped within your desire to not get hurt, that you have to take a chance.

After all, I had come to New York City not just to celebrate *Tracers* and John's big success, but also, deep inside, hoping to find love. Several of the poems I had written at the cottage had been about how women would smile at me but would never want to go home with me, and when it came to getting physical, I felt as if they didn't really see me as a sexual being. The whorehouses I'd visited with Charlie in Mexico, along with my first love, a Princeton graduate and self-professed Communist revolutionary, Carol Blakely, who I had met at an antiwar demonstration in LA, were my first sexual experiences as a paraplegic.

I hadn't made love with anyone in a long time and it was causing me a great deal of stress. The nights I screamed into my pillow at the cottage out of sheer sexual frustration had subsided a bit with the excitement of traveling to New York and meeting up with John and the cast of *Tracers*, but I soon began to feel those tensions building up again. Part of me still felt a need to punish myself for what happened in Vietnam, while another part was desperately struggling to be free of all the guilt and shame. The process of writing *An American Elegy* had at least in part helped me to come to terms with it, and I hoped that maybe, just maybe, there could now be a chance for love.

John and I arrived at the theater at six thirty p.m. that evening and met several actors and actresses, all seeming happy to see us. Built in 1912, the People's Theater was one of those iconic off-Broadway relics with musty smells, dilapidated seats, reeking of the past, yet filled with a fascinating history and a million different stories. This intimate little theater was a lot smaller than Joseph Papp's Public Theater; there couldn't have been more than fifty seats.

As the lights dimmed and the curtain rose, my stomach tightened. The audience was small that night, just a few people scattered here and there. The name of the play was *Homecoming* and the Playbill said it was about veterans' struggles to adjust upon their return home from Vietnam. Certain scenes seemed to have been written by someone who had never been to the war, using worn-out phrases and lacking the artistic integrity of *Tracers*. Even so, John and I laughed and enjoyed the play. It had a campy side too that had us both cracking up—partly the way you might enjoy a B movie, but it was also a welcome break from the seriousness of *Tracers*.

Despite its clichés, some of the scenes did hit home. One dealt with a returning vet suffering from PTSD and how that affected his relationship with his wife. John laughed uproariously and I could not help but think of his own tumultuous relationship with his wife Lupe, and their constant bickering—though they loved each other very much. John told me they had come close to divorcing several times but always ended up staying together. There was another scene with a veteran completely flipping out and threatening suicide. Another had a naked veteran hiding in a tree, and later sleeping with a loaded gun under his pillow.

So few people back then seemed willing to talk about what our homecoming had been like. There were a few books and movies, but *Tracers* was one of the first plays to break through. And that night at the People's Theater in Greenwich Village, as silly and superficial as *Homecoming* seemed to be, it was still an important step toward Vietnam veterans and America healing from the war.

There were several attractive women in the cast, and I hoped I'd get a chance to meet them. I was grateful that the actors were trying to understand what we had been through, and while my main goal was to find love, I was also curious if they had gained any insights into our experiences. When the lights finally came on and the cast appeared for their final curtain call, John and I applauded vigorously.

We met several of the actresses afterward, and John and I congratulated them. They were grateful that we had come down that night. An actress named Janet told me that we were, as far as she knew, the first Vietnam veterans to attend their performance.

One actress in particular caught my eye. Her name

was Mona and I was instantly drawn to her. She told me she was an English professor at Hunter College and had read *Born on the Fourth of July*, and loved it. She went on to explain that all of her students were now reading it, and I was both flattered and impressed. Her cute Irish face reminded me of my mother's, especially her pretty upturned nose and sparkling brown eyes. She wore a short black leather skirt and was beautiful enough to be a model.

There was a bit of sarcasm and intensity about Mona that I could relate to and found quite compelling. I hadn't met a woman with such a way with words in a long time; not since Kitty Jennings at Kent State had I spent time with anyone so verbally sharp. There was sassiness about Mona too, a provocative, almost testy nature, like she was feeling me out and challenging me at the same time. It was quite frankly similar to the way *I* was with people—sizing them up before I got to know them. Mona also had a bit of a shifty quality about her; right away I felt it—a look in her eyes, a feeling that I couldn't quite trust her. There seemed to be something hidden behind everything she said, something phony about her that somehow drew me to her, like a moth to a flame. And like many young performers, Mona was clearly hell-bent on success.

As we continued our conversation, I learned that she had been spoiled by her father, who had lavished gifts upon her. She was his little princess, as she described it, and she seemed deeply troubled by his death at a relatively young age. She still had a problem talking about it. I asked her questions in that intense way of mine that often turned women off, but not Mona, who seemed to thrive on it. She was charming and frightening, delightful and cunning. I was certain I had never met anyone quite like her.

It was getting late and almost all the actors had left when Mona asked me if I'd like a ride back to my hotel. I immediately agreed and my heart started racing. John had already headed out with one of the other actresses. Mona and I left the theater and I transferred into the passenger seat of her battered pink Pinto, then closed up my chair and with Mona's help placed it in the back-seat.

As Mona sat down in the driver's seat, her short skirt hiked up to her thighs and I got really excited. It was one of those hot summer nights in New York City where time stops and anything seems possible, even love with someone you've just met. She hit the gas and we raced down the streets, barreling through one red light after another, Mona seeming completely oblivious to the law. I rolled down my window and closed my eyes, leaning back in my seat.

"Are you hungry?" she asked, as she pulled into a parking lot in front of a little pizza place on the out-skirts of Hell's Kitchen.

"I'm starving," I responded. "I'll buy if you fly."

She squirmed in her seat and her skirt inched up even higher. As she stepped out of the car, she wiggled her rear end in my face. "Christ," I mumbled under my breath, wondering if she had any idea how crazy she was making me. I was in New York City with a beautiful and sexy actress named Mona; this was so much better than being stuck in the cottage in Sausalito trying to write the Great American Novel and feeling so miserable.

We gobbled up our pizza, and before we knew what was happening, we began making out. It was not the tender kissing of new lovers, but fierce and explosive, as if we were attacking each other, tearing at each other's bodies. All those lonely nights in the cottage, all those angry poems about a man who had begun hating the world because he couldn't find love—now, here I was in Hell's Kitchen, finally releasing my pent-up sexual frustration, driving it deep into Mona's mouth with my tongue, ripping her blouse and squeezing her tits so hard that she cried for me to stop; all that frustration that had gone into hundreds of paintings and short stories, all the desperate, lustful yearnings for pretty young women but never going home with one of them.

Mona and I continued making out as we headed back to the Edison with her black leather skirt now hiked all the way up, her blouse unbuttoned to her waist, her pantyhose down to her ankles, both of us sweating profusely. "Oh God," she moaned, "you have to stop—I can't drive. I can't drive!"

My face was still drenched in sweat, my heart pounding in my chest, when we reached the Edison. I transferred into my wheelchair and Mona pushed me into the lobby. As we rode the elevator up to the seventeenth floor, we were like wild animals, she ripping the buttons off my shirt, me clawing her silk blouse to shreds. There was a recklessness to our lovemaking that night, as if nothing mattered anymore, just the penetration of this woman by any means necessary; with my tongue, with my finger, with my elbow, with anything that would get into her cunt or stick into her mouth. It was as if those moments on the bed were the wildest moments of my life. She was all the women I had ever wanted, all those frustrations, all those years, all those pent-up emotions, repressed sexual needs pouring out of me like a dam bursting, like a volcano exploding, like a flash flood in all its ferocity and damaging fury.

I was finally fucking for all that loneliness, fucking for all those lost and angry years, fucking for the girls who wouldn't go out with me, fucking for all the ones who did but wanted penises and needed them hard, fucking for the blondes and the brunettes, the tall ones and short ones, the fat ones and skinny ones, for all the tight skirts and wiggling little assess, for all those horny thoughts and dreams, all those legs spread wide apart like those erotic drawings I had done in Jacques's apartment in Paris; all those cunts drawn with a pencil, all those enormous oversized penises bulging in the American night, screaming for deliverance, crying out for love; *all* those aching frustrating nights and days, that eternity of sexual frustration, of cultural stupidity, of idiotic ignorant women and men who could not think beyond the rod, the pole, the poker, who did not know that fingers were penises too; the way it had been in my dream at the Edison Hotel that night.

Perhaps Anaïs Nin was right when she said that

sex was in need of a new language, a new definition. Perhaps there was still hope for me, still a chance to accept myself sexually, to not give up or believe what they would like me to believe—that it was over and done with forever, dead as a doornail, crushed and crucified, castrated and clobbered, put in cold storage—yet something deep within told me there were other ways to make love, other more creative approaches yet to be explored, other than the one that I and so many others of my generation had been taught and conditioned to believe.

I now began to see that my loss, that devastating savage loss of my private parts, my penis, my manhood, was not the end of sex but perhaps the beginning of a new understanding, a new language of what sex was really all about; not one penis, one pole, one hole, one thrust and penetration, one moan and groan, but the penetration of every cell, every inch of skin and fiber, the nose and ears and eyes and lips and tongue, my fingertips, my breath and her breath, the simple interaction of two bodies dancing in the sun, two cheeks pressing tenderly against each other on that warm summer night.

To know that there was more to it than just the clit, or the penis that touched the clit, that there was a clit to every part of the human body, a clit to the nose, the ears, the warmth and delightful smell of her breath, her body against mine—to stick it in, to pull it out, the whole maddening idea of performance now seemed absurd to me. Performing what? As if people were supposed to cheer when a man chopped a block of wood, or a woman sawed a log in half.

We had only just begun to understand what making love was really about, how people had made love in that crude, simplistic-archaic fashion for centuries—the desperate need to perform, to please, sticking the penis inside the vagina, speaking words they didn't really mean, caught up in the heat, the lust of the vile act itself, the temporary rush, the thrill of the fuck, like the thrill of winning an Olympic gold medal. There were more things than the cunt and the penis which had been raised to godlike status, put on a pedestal and worshipped for centuries.

Because he had lost his penis in the war, he could now clearly see how important it was to keep his mind open and to challenge what others continued to see as impossible, outlandish, and unattainable. In Paris, he had begun to discover new ways of dealing with his sexual loss, new and exciting approaches to feeling a part of a world that he had once felt so isolated and estranged from. He was figuring ways to come back in, to be a part of everyone else again, to reclaim his sexual identity and his identity as a human being.

Having been raised in a lower-income family and having been forced to go to summer school after my last year of high school because of my poor grades, it was quite a step up to be going out with an upper-class woman who had graduated from a prestigious college. Perhaps it was my deep insecurity and working-class shame, never spoken, but always just below the surface, that drew me toward Mona, reminding me of high school when those arrogant, cocky, well-dressed girls from the other side of the tracks would strut around during study hall in their haughty, sexy manner, reeking of class confidence, taunting and teasing us.

The rage that had built up during those lonely nights in the cottage, when I had screamed into my pillow for relief, was now coming out with Mona. I was kissing her wildly, as if there were no tomorrow, swirling my tongue around in her mouth, pushing it in like a penis; asserting myself, yes, letting my tongue become my erection, my manhood; pushing, prodding, poking it into her mouth like it was her vagina; kissing her until my lips bled, wanting to let her know that even without my penis, I was still a man and not some eunuch or inferior being. *I'm somebody!* I seemed to be screaming. *This is who I am, the full and complete man, not half a man but a whole man, a whole person right here and now with my tongue and my hands and my arms and my chest and this one nipple that I can still feel!*

Finally, at around three a.m., she left, telling me she had to teach a class the next day. My heart was still pounding in my chest as I closed my eyes and slept.

Mona and I started seeing each other every day after that. She was constantly on my mind, and instead of going to *Tracers* and spending time with John and the others, I began going to every performance of *Homecoming*, ending each night with her in my bed at the Edison.

I couldn't believe how down I felt when Mona wasn't around or wasn't able to come over to the hotel for our nightly rendezvous, and then when she finally did show up I'd be flying high as a kite after making love with her.

And each time it got more intense, as if the dose had to be increased so that I could keep enjoying myself.

That's what I felt when I wheeled down those streets in Times Square, taking her to the subway, pulling her toward me, making out with her while people walked around us, not caring at all what they thought or said, just completely fixated on this one person, this one face, locked into this woman as if she was the only thing in the world that mattered to me anymore. I would then watch her walk down those subway steps, my heart and paralyzed penis reaching out to her as she strode toward the turnstiles; watching her cute little ass in her short skirt, her high heels clicking away madly, thinking to myself, *I just fucked that woman. We just made love. I'm in love with that crazy fucking woman,* yet feeling frightened that I was feeling so good, so happy, wondering if all of this might end and I might come crashing down the way my friend Waldo the screenwriter had predicted.

> *I will sit in this hotel room and write love poems to you.*
> *That will be my sole obsession, my job in life, my work,*
> *as my father once worked.*
> *I will dedicate my typewriter to you, the woman I love,*
> *the woman I had sex with last night, the woman who*
> *I have been writing about all afternoon.*
> *I will wait for you to come tonight, to share my bed*
> *with me, to kiss me one more time, afraid already you*
> *are beginning to realize how in love with you I am.*

I couldn't get Mona out of my mind no matter how

hard I tried, no matter what I did or where I went. She started coming over to the hotel during her lunch break from school. She'd catch a cab to the Edison and we'd make love. I felt a little resentful that she never seemed to want to make love at her own apartment. I kept waiting for her to invite me to her place for that dinner she always promised she'd cook for me, but she seemed to make a lot of promises she didn't keep, always telling me not to worry and that later, later, always later . . . She was always so busy. She was always so sorry. *Not tonight, maybe next week.*

She seemed to be stringing me along, hustling me, but I couldn't do anything about it. I was "hooked," as my friend Richard Boyle had once called it, and I had swallowed the hook whole. I was babbling about her in my sleep at night, always waking up thinking about her, taking my daily shower in the sink thinking about her, painting thinking about her, typing thinking about her.

Every day when I called her on the phone, my heart would start pounding and I'd start sweating, always afraid she might reject me. Richard Boyle once said that there were two things that kept you from leaving a place: one was a lack of "bread," and the other was a woman who had hooked you. And at that point I don't think I could have left New York City even if I had wanted to.

Raindrops on the Moon

in this simple room
on this simple table

i will write this poem
i hear Spanish voices out my window
"Leave it alone!" they say
i hear sirens too
the City is out there
great buildings all around
blue sky and sunshine
things to do
boxing matches
trips to Massapequa
plays and sex
i am in love
with the woman in the dress and the pretty smile
the actress, the teacher
who says we will be together forever
i saw so many hearts broken in my lifetime
so many hopes and dreams shattered
that to believe what this woman is saying to me
to accept that this all could be
is as difficult
as the thought of trying to hear
the sound
of raindrops on the moon

A FOOL FOR LOVE

Mona began coming to the hotel later and later, always with an excuse. She'd stagger in, exhausted, and plop herself onto my bed. Before I'd have a chance to transfer out of my wheelchair to make love, she'd be fast asleep. Who was this strange person sleeping next to me, snoring so loud I couldn't sleep? It started to dawn on me that I was a fool, making myself vulnerable the way I had with other women, making a complete ass of myself.

Soon, we were screaming and fighting all the time. She refused to accept flowers I gave her one afternoon, tossing them in the garbage. I felt angry and sad, thinking again about leaving the United States, remembering what a guy in the Edison bar had said to me one night about getting out of America before he had a breakdown over a woman he was seeing.

Maybe it was already too late, maybe I should have gone to Bermuda with that guy in the bar before things got so bad with Mona, before all the terrible fighting and vicious things that were now being said. When I told her one night that going out with her was worse than Vietnam, she just laughed at me.

Then she started visiting me at the hotel less frequently, telling me she was busy with school or that she had to rehearse her lines for a new play. I suspected she was cheating on me and I thought about Richard Boyle's warning that the "green-eyed monster of jealousy" could drive a man crazy.

Everything seemed to be coming unglued. I was afraid to close my eyes at night, afraid I would never awaken from the darkness. On the intensive care ward in Vietnam, I had been given morphine shots every four hours to make me sleep. They had to literally knock me out. And after I left the VA hospital in the Bronx, that same vicious pattern returned of insomnia each night and anxiety attacks each morning. While there had been periods of relative relief, this torment was never far away. And now, here it was again: each morning upon awakening, I would feel a wild panic and would desperately climb into my wheelchair, pushing myself to the bathroom toilet bowl and sticking my finger down my throat until I retched. Then in the afternoon I would have another anxiety attack.

I had come to New York City hoping to escape the loneliness and isolation of the cottage, and now here I was, having not slept in days, staring like a zombie out my seventeenth-floor window.

The Psychiatric Ward

When I entered the psychiatric ward, I immediately noticed a framed self-portrait of Vincent van Gogh on the wall above the nurse's station. *That's interesting,* I thought to myself. Here, of all places, a locked psychiatric ward at a VA hospital in Manhattan, they seemed to be showing respect and compassion for this troubled artist. *Maybe they'll understand me. Maybe this is not such a frightening place,* I remember thinking as a sense of peace swept over me.

The psychiatrist I met with told me he had just read *Born on the Fourth of July,* and found it fascinating. "Thank you," I mumbled, as the tension that usually exists between doctor and patient began to break down. I had not expected this. As we spoke, I realized he was not feeling sorry for me, nor was he treating me like a victim. On the contrary, he was treating me with respect. He seemed to take it for granted that sensitive and creative people will sometimes end up on psychiatric wards, just like Tennessee Williams and Eugene O'Neill had.

After he left I felt a bit stronger, as if I had gotten a part of my identity back—the pride and sense of self-worth that my terrible fights with Mona had taken away. Regardless of another failed romance, I still had a responsibility to express myself and keep touching the lives of others. I needed to keep speaking at high schools, colleges, churches, at demonstrations, wherever people would listen to me. It was important that I show as many people as possible what the war had done to me—not only speak it but write it as honestly as I could.

I did my best to adjust to my new surroundings, determined to get with the program, the way I had on my first day of boot camp at Parris Island and as a patient at the Bronx VA hospital. Knowing how to act in an institutional environment can be crucial to one's survival. If you don't go along with the program, things can get very difficult. I had learned the same thing in jail and other places: you have to become a part of everything happening around you, in sync with the whole situation. Don't rock the boat—not because you believe in it or you respect the regulations and boundaries, but because you simply want to survive.

There was a time and a place for protest, for raising your voice, for shouting and screaming and shaking your fist, but once you were inside their institutions—whether Marine Corps boot camp, the LA County Jail, or the psychiatric ward in a VA hospital—the rules were no longer the same. Once they had you behind those steel doors and wire windows, it was a whole different ball game. If you were lucky enough to get out of the place alive, then you could play by your own rules again. "You don't rebel on the inside," Richard Boyle once told me.

I remember one of the aides helping me put on my government pajamas, making sure I didn't have any sharp objects—pens, pencils, etc. It must have been close to midnight when he pushed me back into the ward where everyone was already asleep. After I transferred into my bed, I was grateful to finally sleep, even if I had to resort to sleeping pills, something I'd promised myself I would never do, knowing full well the risk of addiction. I lay in bed awake for several hours the next morning before finally transferring back into my wheelchair as others started getting up all around me.

> *Who are these? Why sit they here in twilight?*
> *Wherefore rock they, purgatorial shadows,*
> *Drooping tongues from jaws that slob their relish,*
> *Baring teeth that leer like skulls' tongues wicked?*
> —"Mental Cases" (1920) by Wilfred Owen

LOCKED STEEL DOORS
AND WIRE WINDOWS

As I looked at all the broken men around me, I wondered what the presidents would have thought if they were still alive and could walk into this place. *Here's your New Frontier, Mr. President, impaled on all those hopes and dreams, pissing in their bedsheets, crying out in a grief they cannot express. Here is your war on Communism and crusade against the Reds. Here's your Great Society in ashes. Here's your "noble victory" and "honorable peace," lost in a lithium haze, staggering down the hall on Thorazine. "Yet, were they not blind too?" whispers a sightless man alone in his room.*

Is it that we are the prisoners inside this place or are we the free ones, the few human beings who have the courage to admit our pain, to confess our sorrow, the few who have been willing to cry out, like Eddie, who continues to weep unashamedly as he stares through the wire windows of the psychiatric ward's steel door. *Perhaps we are not the crazy ones,* I think, *the ones to fear. Perhaps we are the fortunate ones, being protected here from the real danger out there, and this place is but a brief respite from all that madness.*

Everyone knows what's going on here. Nobody says it openly, none of the nurses or doctors. They seem to respect us because we have been willing to say what almost everyone else does not want to say; the way Hopkins did, and Tom and Marty and Max and all the rest. Yet still we continued on, brothers of this madness, victims of this idiocy, ghosts like shadows acting out a play that will never be written.

Even with all the humiliation and shame of having to turn myself in to a place like this, I could not help but feel that I had finally come home; the way I felt when I visited the Vietnam Memorial in Washington, DC, and sat before the names of the dead, all that death carved into stone. The "Wall" should have been extended for all the psychiatric casualties, for all the people like Tony and Jim and countless others who died and were buried behind these locked steel doors and wire windows.

The staff at the psychiatric ward use an assortment of drugs to keep us all in line. I remember one guy, an extremely agitated former Marine Corps drill instructor named Billy, who had served two tours of duty in Vietnam and received a Silver Star, telling me he was going to become the president of the United States someday. He began explaining in great detail how he planned to go about reaching his goal. Then, five minutes after receiving his medication, he could no longer remember who he was, and all he wanted to do now was fly to Alabama and go fishing. "I used to fish with my father when I was a boy," he told me, staring off into the distance. "I loved fishing with my dad, but after Vietnam I told him I didn't want to go fishing anymore. I was sick and tired of killing. I said, *Dad, the only way I'm going to fish with you again is if we don't use any hooks*. He agreed and we've been fishing together now for years without hooks . . . I'm going to go to sleep now," he said, staggering down the hall in his rumpled pajamas.

So now here I was in a place I had feared for so long. I had finally made it to the loony bin, a locked psychiatric ward at the Manhattan VA hospital. It was quiet, deceptively quiet, with its drab green walls and antiseptic smell. Some of the veterans around me had looks on their faces that seemed completely out of this world, while others seemed shocked from some trauma buried deep inside them that they might never be able to express. There were screams at night and patients howling during the day for reasons I never knew. One veteran with tears streaming down his face kept walking past me whispering, "Incoming! Incoming!" and appeared to be lost in some faraway place he might never return from.

I overheard various conversations in the visiting room, some men talking about how they wanted to go home, others apparently quite satisfied with being on the psychiatric ward, as if it was one of the nicest places in the world. Tony kept telling his mother he wanted to die. Jimmy just sat there staring at his girlfriend like she didn't exist. Eddie said to his mother that he wished he'd never joined the marines, and that if he had to do it again he would have become a priest, and how during his second tour of duty he'd held his dying buddy in his arms and ever since then had felt guilty that he'd survived. "Sometimes I just don't feel like I deserve to be here, Mom," he muttered. "I mean, I'm glad I made it home, but a part of me feels like I already died." His mother started crying.

As the hours passed, I could not help but think how these men I had come to know as my brothers represented millions of other Vietnam veterans out there; and how countless psychiatric wards across the country had to deal with the psychological effects of that war; and what about the families, the mothers, the fathers, the sisters, the brothers, like my mother who became an alcoholic after I came home? She never told me about it. I wouldn't find out about it until years later, when she finally explained how she had started drinking again while I was a patient at the Bronx VA hospital from all the guilt she felt about my paralysis and how she thought it was her fault because she had told me to go fight the Communists.

Mona, who had resisted allowing me to spend even one night at her place, now seemed ready to make all sorts of concessions. She showed up one afternoon behind the wire window and told me that after giving it a lot of thought and talking to some of the other members of the cast, she had decided to let me move into her apartment as soon as I got out of the psychiatric ward. She seemed sincere and promised to bring me a key to her place the following day.

I smiled and thanked her, doing my best to appear grateful. But to be honest, all I could feel was anger and contempt. *Great*, I thought to myself, *I can finally move into your fucking place now that I've been locked up in this crazy house.* She left very quickly after that, telling me she had to get back to the Village for another performance. I just sat there watching her walk away, her Gucci heels clicking on the floor so loud that I came very close to screaming.

November 1985

The most important thing was that I had escaped from the psychiatric ward and they hadn't gotten me to confess. I knew what would probably have happened if I'd stayed there any longer. It would have only been a matter of time before I finally broke down and started spilling my guts, sharing everything that I had been keeping inside me all those years; and once the government got ahold of that information, I imagined they would never let me go.

I awoke the next morning in Mona's apartment in a groggy, doped-up state; I was completely spent. It was an effort for me to get out of bed, and I was amazed that I was functioning at all, given everything I had been through. My whole system seemed to be breaking down physically and emotionally. I fought to right my craft, knowing that if I stopped struggling I would surely slip down into that dark vortex where there would be no coming back, no return to the man I once was. I had to keep moving. I had already survived several devastating defeats, yet I had come back each time like a man possessed; undaunted, I had shown tremendous reserve and battled back with all that was in me, coming close to giving up several times yet refusing to quit. I was operating on pure instinct like some punch-drunk fighter.

Just as I had done on thousands of other mornings since I had come home from the war, I got dressed and threw myself back into my wheelchair, fighting off the deep distress that enveloped me.

By the time I pushed into the living room, Mona had already left for work and I wondered how I had ever gotten involved with this woman in the first place. Her credentials aside, it amazed me how *she* had been able to escape the loony bin. All my belongings were still at the Edison—Mona had called the guy at the front desk and told him that I'd taken a little vacation to Bermuda and would return shortly. My worst fear was that she might tell them the truth. *He's had a nervous breakdown and had to check himself into the psychiatric ward at the VA hospital for evaluation,* I imagined her saying over the phone. *He'll be all right. It's all because of the war, it has nothing to do with our relationship or the fact that I wouldn't let him stay at my apartment because I'm involved with another man who he doesn't even know about.*

I didn't want to go back to the Edison ever again. Because of Mona, the hotel would always provoke sad and painful memories. I would always remember it as the place where I had finally fallen apart, surrendered to the enemy, and turned myself in to the psychiatric ward.

But I had somehow wiggled my way out of the nuthouse before they were able to get me into that rubber room at the end of the hall to break me down, evaluate me, and make me talk, creating a thick file of all my phobias and eccentric behaviors, my mindless wanderings and zany activities after the war; all my crazy friends and rebellious ways; all my sexual fantasies and nightmares, my violent, vengeful thoughts.

Jim was still asleep on the couch and I decided to wake him gently. He had flown in from LA the night before after several desperate calls from me, pleading with him to save me and take me back to the West Coast.

After a few cups of coffee and a big breakfast, I asked Jim if he would be willing to drive me out to my hometown of Massapequa, Long Island, explaining that I needed to return one last time and make peace with that place that had once meant so much to me. He seemed to completely understand and immediately agreed to head out to Massapequa that morning.

Jim pushed my wheelchair through Mona's front door and down the long hallway to the elevator. At the ground floor we headed out into the street where busy New Yorkers hurried past us and Jim pushed me for nearly three blocks to where his rental car was parked. With his assistance, I quickly transferred into the passenger seat and soon we were racing toward the Midtown Tunnel.

MASSAPEQUA

You Can't Go Home Again
—Thomas Wolf

That same feeling of loss and death surrounded him now as he sat among the wreckage of his youth, that awful and helpless feeling that had threatened to overwhelm him; that strange and eerie sense of a witness walking among the dead, like some ghost in a dream or nightmare that would never end.

After the great victory of World War II, there was an explosion like the bursting of a dam and everyone seemed to be getting out of the service at once, and they all wanted to get married and have children and move out to the suburbs; and they couldn't do it fast enough. The Depression and war years were over and now everything seemed possible. Long Island was booming back then, and what had begun as a trickle became a flood. Houses were going up everywhere, reminding people of the Wild West when towns seemed to suddenly spring up overnight. Families poured into Massapequa and shops

and stores were built so fast you couldn't keep up with
them all. The VFW with the cannon out front went up,
followed by Bohack's supermarket, Krisch's Ice Cream
Parlor, and the new JCPenney on Broadway—on land
that had once been inhabited by the Massapequa In-
dians and their chief Takapusha, who a park close to
town is now named for. This land had been cleared;
bulldozers dug great holes that became our basements,
and then came the foundations and the floors we would
walk on.

"We're almost to Massapequa!" I say to Jim, pointing to
the Broadway exit. My heart is beating even faster now,
the way it does whenever I get close to home; there is
just something about this town that has a powerful hold
on me. Maybe my mother was right that it's unhealthy
for me to keep going back after they sold the house and
moved to Florida, yet every spring when it warms up
back east, I get this stirring in my legs and something
deep within calling me back to Massapequa.

The only trip I ever made to see my parents in Florida
lasted just one day. I remember feeling uncomfortable
from the moment I arrived. It was great to see my mom
and dad but I just couldn't get used to their new home,
no matter how hard I tried. They were happy to see
me and went out of their way to make me comfortable,
though it just didn't feel right.

      That first night upon my arrival I could hardly sleep,
and when I finally did, I had a terrible nightmare that

left me exhausted. After breakfast the following morning, Mom and Dad looked hurt when I blurted out that I had to leave immediately. I also said that I loved their new house and was proud that they'd named their street in Florida *Born on the Fourth of July Lane*—but deep down inside I suspected that I would not be going back there ever again.

"There's Doctor Peters's office on the left," I say as the memories come flooding back. I remember when we were kids back in the '50s and doctors were still making house calls. Doctor Peters would come to our house whenever we got sick, carrying his little black medical bag and his stethoscope hanging around his neck. He was a tall man with a very serious look on his face that always made me a bit nervous. I don't remember him ever smiling but he was always there when we needed him, and after a while, like a lot of doctors back then, we thought of him as family, trusting him with our lives and confident he would always make us well.

Doctor Peters took care of Mom when she was pregnant and delivered two of my brothers, and when Mom lost a child at birth, I was in Vietnam and Dad told me it was Doctor Peters who came to the house and sat by my mother's side, doing his best to comfort her and wipe the tears from her eyes. When Dad had high blood pressure after his boss at the A&P threatened to fire him, Doctor Peters prescribed pills so he wouldn't get chest pains and dizzy spells anymore.

And I remember how when I came home from Vietnam, I burned my foot badly in the shower. The water was scalding hot, and because I had lost the feeling of almost my entire body from my mid-chest down, I didn't realize it until it was too late. There were big blisters and soon an infection set in, and it was Doctor Peters who prescribed antibiotics and got me well again.

I was still living in LA when Mom told me that Doctor Peters had died of cancer. It was a long time ago but I think she said a lot of people from the neighborhood went to his funeral, including both of my parents. My mother said they had a new doctor now, a young man in his twenties fresh out of medical school. Mom said he didn't do house calls like Doctor Peters and you had to make an appointment to see him.

"My block is about a mile down Broadway," I say to Jim. "It's on the left, past the traffic light and Charlie's candy store, right after you pass Sparky's barbershop, and that's Toronto Avenue. It's where I grew up and where I left my mom and dad to join the marines right after high school in 1964 and where I came home a few years later paralyzed and in a wheelchair and Dad wheeled me up the ramp he built when I first came home from the veterans hospital.

"Father Cassidy was waiting for me that day to give me Communion just as I was wheeled into the house. I remember my dog Major barking before I even got through the front door and how he jumped into my lap and kept licking my face, seeming really happy to see me, and I remember hugging him tightly, so happy my

old friend had not forgotten me even though I was now
in a wheelchair."

Every time I'd return from California and go back
to the old neighborhood, I'd feel this excitement inside
of me like something was trying to jump out of my body
and run and play the way I did as a kid. It was as if, but
for a brief moment, I was that boy again before the war
who was still in one piece.

As we move slowly down Toronto Avenue, I can
hardly contain my excitement. I look around, searching
for anything familiar. It's been awhile since I was last
here.

There's Jack Philips's house on the left. He had three
children and worked as an accountant in the city. I was
in LA when my mother told me he had committed suicide in his basement. I didn't know him that well, but I
remember talking to him the summer before at one of
our neighbors' barbecues. He was depressed and told
me he was having lots of problems. He had just lost his
job in the city and could no longer afford the property
tax on his house which, he complained, "keeps going
up." He said that he and his family would probably have
to sell their house and move in with his brother in Levittown. He must have felt that he could be really honest
with me. Maybe it was because of my wheelchair or the
fact that he was a Vietnam veteran too. He was very
drunk and kept slurring his words and crying, and whispering in my ear that he wanted to die and was now seeing a psychiatrist in the city who had given him drugs
for his depression and suicidal thoughts. I encouraged

him not to give up and told him that I was having a
rough time too and that there was still a lot to live for.

We finally park the car and Jim and I both get out.
"That's my house," I say proudly with a sigh, "227 Toronto Avenue. I've been coming here ever since my
mom and dad sold the house and moved to Florida. I
just can't seem to leave the place.

"There used to be a weeping willow in the front
yard—right over there," I say, pointing to an open patch
of grass where my father planted it when I was in high
school. I don't know why they cut it down. It was such
a beautiful tree and I remember its delicate branches
swaying in the wind and how when I first came home
from Vietnam I would stare out the living room window remembering how it made me feel peaceful inside. When the new owner cut it down it was not yet
fully grown, and I could not help but feel that something very young and beautiful had died. Each time I
returned to the old house I would look at that empty
patch of ground and feel sad.

We stand in front of the house for a long time, almost as if in a dream. Then, without either of us saying a word, Jim begins pushing me along the sidewalk
toward the back of the house, and I immediately think
of my father and the summer of 1957 when he and
I built that sidewalk. I was eleven years old and I can
still remember dad with his shovel and the sound of
that cement mixer going around and around and the
smell of fresh cement on that hot summer day. If you

look closely you can see our initials, a bit faded over time, but still there etched into the sidewalk: *EK and RK, 7/7/1957.*

Dad may not have been an artist like my mother's side of the family, yet he was still an extremely creative and innovative man, a "builder of things large and small," as he liked to say, whether it was a simple kitchen cabinet at our house in Massapequa, or the barn he helped build during the Great Depression with his brothers on their dairy farm in Wisconsin. He was a hardworking man with seemingly inexhaustible energy who felt as comfortable with his hammer and saw as my grandmother Mary did with her paintbrush and canvas.

As we enter the backyard, I sense things are very different. Even in the short time since my father and mother sold the house and moved to Florida, so much has changed. My favorite tree that I once climbed as a boy is missing; someone must have cut it down too. I know I shouldn't feel this way, yet I cannot help but think that I've been wounded all over again.

And over there—that's where the parallel bars used to be. My father built them with his own hands when I was still in high school, with pipes he bought at the hardware store on Broadway. My brother Tommy and I would often practice for hours, until it got dark, dreaming of making the Olympics someday and winning a gold medal. When I came home from the hospital years ago, I wheeled into the backyard and the parallel bars were still standing and I went up to them, determined to mount them one last time. And somehow, with a gymnastic move that defies description, I hoisted my paralyzed body between those two bars—and for a few brief seconds, with both arms outstretched, I held myself aloft looking out over the entire yard until I could no longer continue. But the parallel bars, like my legs, are gone now too.

There is a pile of freshly cut firewood stacked neatly in what was once my mother's backyard vegetable garden, reminding me of the dead that day who lay neatly stacked in front of the command bunker after being killed in the artillery attack, like frozen statues, their haunting gazes staring blankly into the sky. I take a deep breath. "I remember them all like long-lost friends," I say to Jim as I begin to cry.

Interlude
(sung as an elegiac poem by an all-boys choir)

The boy who had once lived there was lost for all time, dead and buried like so many others who would never be the same and whose lives had been forever changed by the war. Their lives had once been so simple, so tender and devoid of pain, so innocent, so sweet and young.

And as he sat among the wreckage of his childhood, he thought of his father and he saw his mother's face and heard her sweet voice calling out his name, calling for him to come outside and help his father rake the leaves.

There were the sounds of his friends, Richie and

*Bobby and Pete and the rest; each and every one of
them like the weeping sound of night in the inner
recesses of his soul, like a friendship long since past
brought back to life in the place where he had once
lived and his mother and brothers and sisters and father had lived.*

And over there is the great oak tree, once the tallest tree
in the yard, its leaves now wilting, its trunk and bark
ravaged by disease and the passage of time—defiantly it
still stands. Its great branches once reached out, giving
us shade on those hot summer days. As a young boy I
would climb to the very top on cool fall evenings and
look out over the neighborhood and watch the clouds
in their many shapes and forms drift across the Long
Island sky, and when it grew dark I would stare up
into the heavens as the stars flickered on each night. I
have always been fascinated by the stars, a world unto
themselves.

I remember October of 1957. It was the beginning
of the space race when my father and I stood together
in the backyard staring up into the night as we watched
the first satellite, *Sputnik*, move across the sky above
Massapequa, signaling the beginning of a new and daring age of space exploration; and who knew where we
would go next? Like the great explorer Magellan on the
precipice of his adventures centuries ago, we now stood
before the great timeless sea of space.

Just then the new owner comes out into the backyard. "Can I help you?" the man says.

"I used to live here," I respond. "Would you mind if we came into the house and looked around a bit?"

"Sure. I know who you are. I read your book . . . Come on in." The new owner seems to realize what this visit means to me and is more than pleased to accommodate us. We all shake hands. "How are your parents?" he asks.

"They're doing fine," I say, smiling. Jim takes me to the front of the house and helps me up the steps. "There used to be a ramp here," I tell the new owner. "My father built it when I first came back from Vietnam."

"I read about it in your book," he says, smiling back at me. "This is a very famous house!"

As we enter, I look around and things seem very different. I don't know what I was expecting, but this is not the house I grew up in. This is a strange and foreign place. I search for what was once familiar. The crucifix on the wall to the right with the holy water that I would dip into with my fingers and then make the sign of the cross each time I came into the house is gone. The living room where I played for hours with my brothers has changed too. The furniture is all different. I am momentarily confused, yet at the same time clearly understand what has taken place. The house is not mine, and even though all my memories seem erased, I try with all my might to imagine what once was but is no more.

The man's wife now arrives, smiling too. "We love it here!" she says.

"Do you mind if I look around a bit?" I ask them.

"Not at all, be our guest. We know who you are," the man says again.

Perhaps my room at the end of the hallway—the room I grew up in, joined the marines from, and returned home to from Vietnam—might still be the same, and perhaps there will be some semblance of that boy I had once been. But as I enter the room, I immediately see the crib for the newborn baby where my hospital bed had once been. The bedroom walls have been painted a soft pastel color, and in place of the photos of baseball stars Roger Maris and Mickey Mantle now hang framed portraits of two giraffes.

I sit in my wheelchair for a long time that afternoon reflecting on what my room used to look like, wondering briefly if the newborn baby will ever know anything about the man who once lived there and the great drama that unfolded in that place. Then I begin to laugh, realizing the absurdity and arrogance of my thinking. The child and its parents will be too busy living their own lives to think of such things.

Jim is waiting in the living room as I push myself forward, wiping tears from my eyes. I look at him, and without saying a word, we both know it is time to leave. I have seen enough, and after we said goodbye to the young couple, Jim grips the back handles of my wheelchair and carefully lifts me down the front steps.

He pushes me across the front lawn and helps transfer me into the front seat of his car. We then drive slowly down Toronto Avenue to the end the block, where we make a right on Broadway and head back to the city.

RETURN TO LA

All I wanted to do now was get away from Mona as fast as I could, and never get involved with an actress ever again. I promised Jim that I was going to take some time off from my "crazy relationships." I told myself that if I could just get back to California, everything would be okay again. California had saved me in the past, always waiting out there with its beautiful Pacific Ocean and warm sunshine to shelter me and help heal me.

After we lifted off the runway at JFK Airport, I held Jim's hand for most of the way across the country, feeling certain that I was never going back to New York City, the place of my great downfall and humiliation.

I can still remember confessing to Jim at twenty thousand feet, squeezing his hand as if he was the only friend I had left in the world. I told him about all the nights I had lain in my bed at the Edison, unable to sleep, obsessed with Mona and reassessing my life. I made a solemn vow to Jim that I was going to change my life, make amends for my wild past, and finally settle down. I had seen the light on the psychiatric ward in

Manhattan and knew that I could never return to the way I had lived before.

It was my Act of Contrition, and Jim, like a Catholic priest, absolved me of all my sins.

It was an agonizing trip, reminding me of the time I came back from Vietnam after my first tour of duty in January 1967, flying almost twelve hours straight from Okinawa to Travis Air Force Base in California. I remember telling Jim that I wanted to live and did not want to end up like so many other Vietnam vets who had not been able to make it back, trapped in that vicious cycle of alcohol, drugs, depression, and pain.

I looked down as we made our final approach into Los Angeles, the great City of Angels spread out like a giant checkerboard of flickering lights. When we finally touched down, I breathed a great sigh of relief. After getting our luggage, Jim and I caught a cab over to the Sea Lodge in Venice, where we checked into our room and went to sleep, Jim lying next to me, with me still holding tightly to his hand.

As crazy as it might sound, Mona and I continued to stay in touch, unable to break the powerful sexual bonds that had held us in each other's grip for so many months. I called her from the Sea Lodge almost every night before I went to bed, and sometimes during the afternoon. Jim kept coming over every day and my friend Pat visited me too, trying her best to give me support.

I couldn't tell Pat everything that had happened in New York. I was afraid to let her know that I ended up on a psychiatric ward and now had to take sleeping pills every night, but I did tell her that I had broken up with an actress and got really fucked up over the whole thing.

Not long after my return to the West Coast, I started going to the newly established Veterans Outreach Center in Westwood, a program for Vietnam vets who needed psychological counseling but were frustrated by the government's endless red tape. Many vets were suffering from PTSD and needed a safe environment outside of the VA hospital that they could trust.

RECKONING

January 1986

I tried desperately to keep myself together during that period, telling myself to just take it one day at a time. At the Veterans Outreach Center, I began seeing a counselor named Ed Jacobs twice a week, a big Black man with a booming voice and a zealot's look in his eyes who reminded me more of a high school football coach or Marine Corps drill instructor than a psychiatric counselor who I hoped could save me.

As far as I was concerned, I was in need of emergency care. I had held everything inside of me for years and now it was all gushing out with an almost uncontrollable fury, like a raging river about to spill over its banks. I felt angry and resentful that I could not see Ed every day. Twice a week was not enough. How was I supposed to have a complete debriefing in two one-hour sessions per week?

I tried to accept Ed's rules, but there was not enough time for everything I had to talk about. There were things I had to say that were screaming to get out of me. Having seen numerous therapists over the years,

I felt like I was constantly adjusting to each new one's approach. Like the others, Ed seemed sure that he knew what was best for me.

I didn't know how much combat Ed had actually seen and wondered sometimes if he had seen any at all. I never asked him about this during our therapy sessions, probably not wanting to threaten the image I had created of this heroic veterans outreach counselor who I imagined had saved so many others like me, and through his self-taught therapeutic methods—part bluster, part power of positive thinking—was going to get me "back in shape," as he put it; Norman Vincent Peale in a drill sergeant's hat.

Yet even in the midst of my breakdown, I could see through Ed's facade. I wasn't completely honest with him either, often leading him on the way I had a lot of other therapists over the years, convinced that none of them could understand the depth of what I had been through and all that had happened in Vietnam.

I was an excellent actor . . . telling therapists how pleased I was to be working with them, how much they were helping me, and sometimes even allowing myself to break down and cry in front of them, secretly wanting them to believe I was making progress.

I still feared that if I returned to the psychiatric ward, the worst would happen to me, like what had happened to my Uncle Paul and others from my neighborhood. I had been deceiving people like Ed ever since I'd come home from the war. Even when I was a kid, I had used my wild imagination to make up stories as a way to divert attention away from my problems.

Eventually, though, Ed began to figure me out and would later say that my whole life had been one "miserable masquerade after the next." I remember, as I sat there listening to him strip me naked and rip away my "masquerade," a slight, sardonic smile slowly crossing my face as if someone had finally broken through and freed me from my self-made prison and I was now finally ready to be honest in ways I had never thought possible before; the flood gates had been opened and I would no longer be afraid.

Ed Falls Asleep

At one therapy session, however, I accused Ed of falling asleep just as I was about to tell him about the night I accidently shot and killed one of my own men. He immediately denied he had been sleeping, claiming that he was simply deep in thought. "You were snoring, Ed," I insisted, but that only seemed to make him more defensive. I chose not to keep pressing the issue for fear of losing him as my therapist, my life preserver in a sea of madness.

I was terrified that I was slipping over the edge and that it was only a matter of time before I would end up back on another locked ward. In the end, I decided to apologize to Ed and simply go along with his lie. As I left his office that day, I admitted to myself that Ed Jacobs was not the great veterans outreach therapist that I'd imagined.

* * *

A psychiatrist at the Manhattan VA had warned me that the sleeping pill Halcion was highly addictive and there could be serious side effects, especially when trying to stop taking it. This was corroborated several years later by the author William Styron in his book *Darkness Visible: A Memoir of Madness*, in which he wrote that Halcion was "responsible for at least exaggerating to an intolerable point the suicidal ideas that had possessed me."

One night I wrote in my diary:

> *I am desperate, sick with a terrible emotional fever raging inside of me, and no one seems to be able to do anything to stop it. My emotional temperature continues to rise and I feel more and more frightened. I don't know what keeps me going. I seem to be walking through a horrifying gauntlet of pain. Wherever I go, wherever I turn, there is no relief, only this constant pain pounding down on me.*
>
> *Something is collapsing inside of me. Everything feels off balance. Each morning I wake up feeling frightened and shaky inside, telling myself to just try to take it one day at a time.*

The full force of my past was now upon me, and nothing, not God, if he existed, could hold back this moment of reckoning. Before falling asleep that night, I scribbled in my diary the words, *Hell is a nightmare—heaven is a dream!* having no idea what this actually meant.

* * *

I understand why people kill themselves. I understand what the breaking point means for those of us who have seen too much. I am at that breaking point now. I am right in the middle of it and it is fierce and agonizing. I am on fire and burning alive and I'm supposed to keep functioning? I understand why they quit, why they decide, even the strongest among them, to put a shotgun to their heads the way Jack Philips did that night in his basement in Massapequa, and Max and Jimmy and all the others.

BREAKDOWN

Of course, all life is a process of breaking down.
—F. Scott Fitzgerald, *The Crack-Up*

March 1986

I scream. I cry, but there is no sound. Words cannot begin to describe how frightened I feel, how afraid I am that I might not make it through this agony. It's as if I was shot up with a bunch of bullets and no one can see the blood spurting out all over the place. I'm trying to plug up the holes but no one seems to understand.

It is not like looking at an open wound or a bedsore, or a man sitting in a wheelchair. Emotional wounds are much more complicated, much more subjective a thing. I wonder if anyone will ever know what I am going through. Maybe this is why there always seems to be a mystery concerning mental illness and soldiers who return home from war.

This is the worst it has been. New York City was bad, but nothing like this. This is getting worse each day. I have to fight to complete the most menial task. I force myself to go through the motions. I seem to be possessed by demons that won't let go. They possess my very soul. They haunt me day and night.

They're deep inside me now like a terrible disease, an illness with no explanation. I write the following words: The tears so deep that wet the soul of dreary drip of hurt that cannot fathom mind or loss or what's more can be worse. *I pin the poem to my shirt pocket, hoping people will notice.*

I am amazed as the hours pass that I'm still alive, still breathing, just like that day in Vietnam when I was pulled off the field of battle and saved by the Black marine. I do not know what keeps me going. I just want to make it through the next minute, the next hour. I just want to live to the end of this day and not go crazy and die. Something is collapsing inside of me.

I decide to call John DiFusco, who is back in LA with some of the cast of *Tracers*, taking a break from the show. He immediately recognizes that I am in serious trouble and tells me he'll be right over with Jim and some of the cast members. When they arrive at my hotel room, I am overjoyed.

"Brothers, it's so good to see you," I say, and begin to cry. "I'm having a rough day."

John moves slowly toward me and I reach for his hand.

"I'm not in Vietnam anymore, am I, John?"

He gives me a warm smile and seems calm, as if he has gone through this with other vets before. I hold his hand tightly and the others join him. In New York I had been their hero, their inspiration, their source of strength, but now they are seeing me for who I really am.

As the hours pass, I begin to feel less alone and think that if I die this afternoon, at least I will die with my brothers around me and not like so many other Vietnam veterans, abandoned in dingy and depressing motel rooms.

It has been an intense afternoon. Everyone looks exhausted. My breathing is labored, my heart still racing but not as wildly as before. I have to make a decision.

I ask Jim if he will take me to the VA hospital in Westwood. "I want to turn myself in to the psychiatric ward," I tell him. "I know they'll put me on a locked ward again, but it doesn't matter. I need help."

I transfer into my wheelchair, almost falling out of bed, then take the sharp objects, a pen and pencil, out of my pockets, the way I did on the psychiatric ward at the Manhattan VA. I'm going in again, giving myself up, surrendering to the enemy, but for some reason they don't seem like the enemy anymore. They're just people who I hope can help me. I'm too tired to do this on my own. I feel so vulnerable, so naked and alone. I hope they don't hurt me. I hope there's someone there who can help me.

STRANGE DAYS

Strange days have found us,
strange days have tracked us down.
—Jim Morrison, The Doors

As I sit waiting with Jim to be checked in at the emergency room of the Wadsworth VA hospital, the television seems to be talking to me, with images of volcanoes erupting and dams bursting. *That's what's happening to me right now!* I think.

I cry in front of the doctor in the admitting room, telling her that I am depressed and have not slept in days. "I need help, I really need help," I repeat as tears roll down my cheeks. She is very understanding, but I am careful when she asks if I've been thinking of taking my life; I know that if I say yes, she will surely commit me to the locked psychiatric ward. So I tell her no, even though I am not sure if I am suicidal. Regardless, I can tell by the look in her eyes that I am one step away from going back to that locked ward.

While waiting for the doctor to complete her report, my mind drifts back to a recent conversation with Lou, a psychologist and Golden Gloves boxing champion from the Bronx who I had run into at the Sidewalk Café in Venice. He told me that what was happening to me was not a breakdown but instead a breakthrough. "Just ride with it, brother," he'd said, as if I were riding some sort of gigantic emotional wave that was about to come crashing down. I had thought I was getting better. I thought the work I was doing with Ed at the Veterans Outreach Center was helping me. But now I was slipping back as if I was in some kind of quicksand and the more I struggled, the deeper I sank.

As I sat next to Jim in the waiting room, I began to wonder if there might just be another way of dealing with my breakdown than surrendering to the "enemy" and turning myself in to the psychiatric ward. And then it suddenly came to me: I would leave the Wadsworth VA and check into the Spinal Cord Injury ward at the Long Beach VA, where no one would have to know what I was going through. I had been a patient there many times over the years, healing bedsores and getting over various illnesses. People there knew me and maybe, if I was lucky, I could secretly ride out my madness there. I wouldn't have to tell anyone about my breakdown in New York. As far as they'd be concerned, I'd be just another paralyzed veteran checking into the ward. I'd be safe, and far from the stigma of ending up on another locked psychiatric ward.

"I changed my mind, Jim. Can you please take me down to the Long Beach VA instead? I think that will be much better for me."

Jim looked at me like I was crazy, then immediately stood up and we were off, racing down the 405 freeway like two madmen, headed to the Long Beach VA.

Out of My Mind

I try my best to make believe I am still with him. I have felt this type of detachment before, but never this strong; never has it lasted this long. I feel like I am not within my own body, that I am outside of myself. I think I know what the expression "out of my mind" means now. I do feel I am outside of my own mind, and it is very strange and frightening, as if I am losing a part of myself, losing control.

I try to explain to Jim what I am feeling but he does not seem to understand. It is as if I am speaking in some strange foreign language that he cannot comprehend. He tries very hard to listen but I can see by the look on his face that what I'm saying doesn't seem to register. I wish he could see inside of my mind and feel what I am feeling at this moment. I wish he could experience what I am going through.

It is difficult feeling sympathy for something you cannot see or understand. Wounds inside the mind seem strange and distant, far away and mysterious; things that we cannot explain or give definition to.

I am deep within an emotional crisis that I cannot fully comprehend. Something has broken inside of me and all I know is that I am lost, very lost and feeling detached from all the people I know and all that was once familiar to me. How long will I be here? I do not know. I sit silently in the front seat of Jim's car no longer wanting to talk about my problems, afraid that I have already made him too nervous as it is. In the midst of my breakdown I am trying to imagine myself well again. Maybe this emotional pain will pass; all these fears that my life is about to end. I must keep trying to find my way back—if there is such a thing as going back now, returning to the man I once was before all of this happened. I am out far in the darkness now, lost at sea on a raft going nowhere, hanging on for dear life.

On a scrap of paper I write the following words:

I am a reporter on a journey through my own madness, chronicling my collapse, detailing my depression, observing my disintegration. I am a passenger of my own psychosis. I am completely out of it, yet I'm still aware of everything that's happening around me.

There are some images from this period that still haunt me to this day, things that happened and things that were said that I know I will never forget.

I couldn't believe I was headed to another hospital. Maybe it was the end of the road, like the TV at the Wadsworth VA admitting room seemed to be telling me. I was extremely alert to everything around me and there seemed to be messages and omens everywhere. Everything I had dammed up inside of me since I came home from the war: killing Wilson and the ambush with kids lying in pools of blood, that young Vietnamese boy with his foot blown off, all those bodies that night in bloody pieces, the old man with his brains hanging out . . .

I had written about this in *Born on the Fourth of July.* It had been the most difficult chapter of the book for me. When my editor had insisted that I write that section, I cursed at her over the phone, but in the end I wrote it and it became one of the most powerful chapters of the book. But I had become so sick and tired of the war, of my editor and the book; I didn't want to write another word. *Fuck them all,* I had thought. *How much more do I have to suffer? How much more do I have to bleed for these people? Do they have any idea what they're putting me through?*

For several nights after writing that chapter, I had terrible nightmares. *I don't ever want to return to that place again,* I thought—but now it had all come roaring back.

DARKNESS

The pain of severe depression is quite unimaginable
to those who have not suffered it, and it kills
in many instances because its anguish can no
longer be borne. The prevention of many suicides
will continue to be hindered until there is a
general awareness of the nature of this pain.
—William Styron, *Darkness Visible:*
A Memoir of Madness

My depression seems to be getting worse. The frightening thoughts have returned again this morning and they are stronger than ever. I feel trapped, completely encased in this thing. I am a prisoner of this nightmare that seems it will never end. *There is only one way out*, a voice screams inside of me, *only one escape from this unending pain!* I try to resist these thoughts, yet the truth is, in some strange way they bring me relief.

As I lie in my hospital bed, groggy from another night without sleep, I begin to formulate a plan to end my life. I go over every detail. In my fantasy, I will leave the hospital and drive my hand-controlled car to Venice, where I will check into the Sea Lodge for the weekend.

Upon my arrival I imagine myself being very upbeat with the guy behind the desk, hiding my deep dark secret. I am exuberant, almost giddy. I have not felt happier or more hopeful in months. Everything around me seems beautiful, so fresh and new. I take a deep breath, feeling a whole new sense of optimism. The darkness and depression that have pursued me for so long seem to have all but disappeared in the knowledge of what I'm about to do. Soon there will be relief, and this thought alone fills me with a tremendous sense of joy. I will check into my room. It will all be over soon. I will bring what's left of my sleeping pills with me. I know exactly what I will do.

As I lie in my hospital bed that morning, I continue to replay my suicidal fantasy over and over in my mind, each time breaking down and crying into my pillow, mourning my death that hasn't happened yet. Later that afternoon, still deeply depressed and feeling as if I am getting closer to turning my fantasy into a reality, I decide to call my friend Pat, desperately hoping she can help me.

For some reason, during our conversation my deep dark secret comes spilling out. Something inside of me, I believe, senses that if I begin openly talking about my plan to kill myself, then maybe I will be able to stop this from happening. Something inside of me still desperately wants to live and not die. I share everything with Pat that afternoon, tears streaming down my face.

It is as if I am at confession telling the priest everything, leaving nothing behind. Pat listens intently to my every word, and when I finish saying all there is to say, she pleads with me to not give up. She reminds me that I still have a lot to live for. "Don't forget who you are, Ronnie," I remember her saying softly from the other end of the phone.

A great battle is going on within me and the sound of her caring voice in this unending sea of pain and darkness has, at least for the moment, kept me from slipping over the edge. In that thin line between life and death, giving up and staying in this world, one voice has made the difference.

Pat patiently listens on the other end of the line, allowing my tears to flow. She tells me that she loves me and will always be my friend. I thank her, still crying. The sound of her voice at least for today has saved me.

A NEW DAWN

Redemption
Tuesday, April 15, 1986

I slowly get dressed, forcing myself through the motions. I fight against the depression, pushing the thought of suicide out of my mind the moment it enters. There must be another way to find relief from all this madness. Maybe that is what this day will bring. Am I feeling hopeful? I don't know. My conversation with Pat yesterday seems to have opened up a new way of seeing things, perhaps a different path from this unending darkness.

Still in a bit of a daze, I leave the ward, pushing my wheelchair out the door and down the hospital sidewalk. As I slowly move along, I notice a bright yellow daisy emerging from a crack in the concrete. The sight of this beautiful yet fragile flower moves me deeply. How amazing that this delicate little flower could find its way through solid concrete. This must be another sign being given to me, another strange and unseen hand helping to guide me.

After studying the daisy briefly, I decide to head toward an opening in the wall that separates the hospital from the university next door. *Two different worlds, I think, one of war and sorrow, the other of hope and new beginnings.*

Years ago, while I was a patient here trying to heal a bedsore, I had first discovered this opening and a world far different from the one I and the others were experiencing on the paraplegic ward. On one of my many visits back then, I discovered a fountain near the campus entrance that was to bring me a sense of inner peace that had been eluding me. I would sit beside its soothing waters, unaware of the passage of time, leaving behind all my fears and sorrows.

Situated in the middle of the pool was what could best be described as a large abstract sculpture. At first glance it appeared to perfectly symbolize my own life back then: completely chaotic with its twisted pipes shooting powerful sprays of water in every direction; though as time went on and my visits to the fountain became more frequent, I began to grasp a deeper meaning in all of its complexity. I thought back to some of the abstract paintings I had done at the cottage and the seemingly absurdist gibberish I had written while struggling to create *An American Elegy*.

As I now approach the opening in the wall, I cannot help but sense that there is something different about this day. I can't explain it but something inside of me can sense a shifting of the tide, the calm before a great storm. Could this be that turning point I imagined years ago in my room in Massapequa when I first came home from the war and felt so hopeless and depressed, wondering if I would ever be able to survive what had happened to me?

I take a deep breath and continue on. As I pass through the wall's opening and enter the university grounds, for some reason today I decide to bypass the fountain. Something compels me to continue along the sidewalk toward the university's main library. Students all around me carry their books and head to class and I think back to my days at Hofstra University on Long Island where I first began taking classes not long after being discharged from the Bronx VA hospital in 1969. What a different world that was from the Bronx VA paraplegic ward and the wounded bodies all around me.

As I move along, I begin to see symbolic meaning in everything. A great oak tree to my left catches my gaze. Its ancient roots lie naked above the ground, totally exposed, its history of growth and pain in every twist and turn clinging to the earth like ancient fingers desperately wanting to live.

Is what I have been going through, all this pain and sorrow, nothing more than a changing of seasons of sorts, a shifting of the tide within me from winter to spring and not the dreaded cold of death that I have for so long feared?

Could this day possibly represent a new beginning, a bursting forth in bloom of something new rather than the ending of all that I have known? Perhaps, I think, something is not dying as much as something new is about to be born. How strange a journey, not into darkness and death but toward light and hope and a new beginning, where all the jumbled pieces and scattered thoughts will be fit together, where meaning and balance will be given to all things both past and present.

The summer sun is setting, heading into fall, and the fall into winter so dark and cold, seeming as if it will never end, yet in the spring cometh rebirth.

A Strange Vision

Above the large building that is the library there is much commotion. I look up and there appears to be a great struggle going on between a group of black crows and perhaps six or seven tiny sparrows. The sparrows do somersaults in midair, trying to avoid the crows following their every move. The sparrows are clearly outnumbered and I fear they will soon be overwhelmed.

As I sit and watch the chase unfold in the sky above me, it grows darker. Is it night or is it day? Is this another sign I am witnessing, perhaps a vision of what is to come, or is this nothing more than an indication that I have finally lost my mind?

There is now darkness all around me as I sit here alone in eerie silence, piercing the wind. I hold on tightly to my chair. I look up. Something strange is happening in the sky above me. The crows have turned into hawks and the sparrows into doves and it appears the hawks are winning. Perhaps this is another sign, I think, that I am to be involved in a great struggle between war and peace and that all my life up until now, all that I have suffered, all that I have gone through, has led me to this place.

The Dark Night of the Soul

But now I hear a strange voice that at first startles me. It begins as a whisper, then grows in intensity until I can clearly make out the words. It is a voice filled with foreboding and grave concern. It speaks of a time of great danger for America, which the voice warns still lies ahead. It speaks of the dark night of the soul of a nation, a ship without a rudder, a craft adrift, lost in a sea of madness and sorrow, with no compass to steer its way. Could my mother's dream that I was to become the man of my generation and a leading figure in my country's destiny be true? Could what I first believed to be a humiliating defeat, a loss and shame beyond all shame, have actually been a blessing in disguise, preparing me for the role that I am soon to play in the time which still lies ahead? Am I being given a look into the future, the meaning of this journey, this great and agonizing puzzle that has been my life?

Blessed are the peacemakers for they shall be called the children of God, the voice now whispers softly in my ear.

Is this that I have been experiencing today in this place a message from God? But how could it be when I'm so sure that God does not exist, that God is dead— or is he?

As I continue staring up into the sky above me, the darkness lifts, and a new dawn begins. It is becoming brighter and brighter until I can no longer see the hawks and the doves. All around me I now hear the voices of students heading to class. The world has returned and the gentle scent of spring sweeps across my face. The harsh winds of my past, so biting and cruel, have now subsided. *Perhaps they are gone forever,* I think.

I slowly wheel back toward the opening in the wall, exhausted yet in some strange way feeling renewed. I have had a powerful vision today and it has affected me deeply.

Just as I am about to pass through the opening, I hear the university's bell tower chiming in the distance. It is the New Year's song, "Auld Lang Syne," signifying a farewell to the old and a welcoming in of the new. How strange, I think, that this song should be playing now.

As I push my wheelchair back toward the paraplegic ward, I cannot help but sense that a great burden has been lifted. The awful depression and sorrow that have consumed me for so long seem to have now all but disappeared. No longer do I feel as if I am dying.

Like a snake that has shed its skin only to be reborn into a new life, I too have shed my skin of the past. Something has changed within my very soul and my faith has been restored. There has been a reckoning, a renewal. My paralyzed body will always be there, a living reminder of that war, but it has also become something beautiful now, something of faith and hope and love. I have been given the opportunity to move through that dark night of the soul to a new shore, to gain an understanding, a knowledge, an entirely different vision.

The one gift I was given in that war was an awak-

ening. I became a messenger, a living symbol, a man
who learned that love and forgiveness are more powerful than hatred; who learned to embrace all men and
women as my brothers and sisters. No one will ever
again be my enemy; no government will ever teach me
to hate another human being. I have been given the
task of lighting a lantern, ringing a bell, shouting from
the highest rooftops, warning the American people and
citizens everywhere of the deep immorality and utter
wrongness of this approach to solving our problems.

Those of us lucky enough to have survived the
homecoming after the trauma of our injuries yearn for
life now, for beauty and all that is decent and good, for
in war we saw the worst in human beings. We saw pov-
erty and death, killing and savagery, the darkest sides of
the soul, the most hated parts of our humanity.

We who have taken our wounds and our sorrows
and chosen to make them stand for something better
have an obligation to rise above our pain and anguish,
to turn the tragedy of our generation into a triumph
and learn from the errors of our fathers and ourselves.
For it is we who have walked and wheeled through the
streets of our country and watched children stare at us
and wonder why. And it is we who cry out now for the
future, for a world without war. We are the reminders
of what war can do.

No one knows peace or the preciousness of life better than those who fought in war, or those who have
been affected by it directly—a mother whose son has
died, a wife who will never see her husband again, a

child who will never have a father, a father who will never see his son.

I am very grateful to be alive, and recently I bought a piano. I love to play the high notes, they are gentle and soothing, almost like the sound of raindrops on my window when I was a boy. Just to touch the keys from time to time helps me to forget the war. The music of the piano fills the air with healing. The past recedes. And sometimes even the nightmares disappear for a while.

The sound of a single note gives hope. Somehow, we must begin to find the courage to create a better world, even if it is with just one note or one step.

The End

Acknowledgments

First, I'd like to thank my publisher and editor, Johnny Temple, who stood by the book from the very beginning. His brilliance, enthusiasm, and exceptional gift as an editor made the book what it is today. It was a joy to work with him.

Thanks also to Johanna Ingalls at Akashic Books, who took the time to listen and proved to be invaluable toward the final completion of the book. And to Aaron Petrovich and Holly Watson for their work to bring this to the public.

Thank you to my loyal assistant, Kris Lynch, for his consistent help and support each day.

And a special thanks to Estella Morones, for her joyful presence, laughter, and smile.

And lastly, I want to thank my dear sweet love, TerriAnn Ferren, who believed in this book from the very beginning and insisted that my Vietnam diary should open it. Her exceptional intelligence and judgment helped make the book what it is today. You, my love, have been a consistent source of inspiration, love, and support. Clearly, *A Dangerous Country: An American Elegy*, one of the most difficult and challenging books of my life, could never have been written without you.